THE
LITTLE ISLAND
BAKE SHOP

JANA ROERICK

Vancouver / Berkeley

THE LITTLE ISLAND BAKE SHOP

Heirloom Recipes
Made for Sharing

FOR MY SON, KYLE, WHO
IS BECOMING A GREAT CHEF
IN HIS OWN RIGHT

Cataloguing data is available from Library
and Archives Canada
ISBN 978-1-77327-063-0 (hbk.)

Design by Jessica Sullivan
Photography by DL Acken
Food and prop styling by Aurelia Louvet

Editing by Michelle Meade
Copy editing by Pam Robertson
Proofreading by Grace Yaginuma
Indexing by Iva Cheung

Printed and bound in China by C&C Offset Printing Co., Ltd.
Distributed internationally by Publishers Group West

Figure 1 Publishing Inc.
Vancouver BC Canada
www.figure1publishing.com

CONTENTS

RECIPES

A NOTE FROM A BAKER

I'VE COME TO REALIZE that the best thing about baking is making people happy. It humbles me to know that something I have made with love has the power to comfort, lift moods and trigger nostalgia. I get immense satisfaction and reward from seeing others enjoy my recipes.

Baking, you see, is as much about feeding someone's heart and soul as it is about nourishing their body. It's science and it's art, but it's also kindness and generosity. Have you noticed that you never bake something for just one person? Whether it's a pie or a tray of cookies, baking is always meant to be shared.

My baking isn't fussy. It's classic and crave-worthy, good and good for you, which is why most of these recipes are lower in sugar and can easily be made gluten-free (page 24). And even though I'm a trained pastry chef, you don't need to be one to make these recipes—most, if not all, are as accessible as they are delicious.

People say my baking is the best they've ever had, and they ask: What is it that makes it so fantastic? It's too corny to say that there's love in it, but there's love in it.

JANA ROERICK

ISLAND TREATS

IT STARTED WITH a bike, a bell and a cart full of home baking.

When I was growing up on the Toronto Islands, every Friday my mom and I would start baking pies, cookies, squares and muffins. By Saturday afternoon we'd have enough to load up our wooden cart and head out on the streets of Ward's Island. We'd ring an old school-bell, and islanders and visitors alike would rush to buy our baking. We'd always sell out.

Growing up, I was surrounded by a community of bakers who make the sort of comforting confections that people love best. I inherited the baking bug from my mom, Barbara (who gave me my very first apple pie lesson), my Granna and my dad. Even though my father passed when I was very young, I can still remember his bran muffins and pancakes.

Naturally, I always knew I wanted to be a professional baker. I was twenty-three and had just had my son, Kyle, when I decided to become a pastry chef. I wanted to understand the science behind baking, and that's what guided me to George Brown College.

I enrolled in the apprenticeship program as a novice, which meant I had to have a special interview to be accepted. I still remember how intrigued my professor was by my story of selling baked goods from the cart. I was accepted to the program with smiles. I was a big kid in a class of young guns who showed me the techniques of the trade so I could keep up. I continued on to Bakers Advanced and Patissier, graduating with honours. I loved the experience and especially my newfound knowledge. Still, it would take me many years to feel accomplished enough to call myself a pastry chef. There is just so much to learn.

My apprenticeship at Dufflet Pastries in Toronto gave me good insight into mid-sized production and the importance of preparation. After that, a brief stint at Wanda's Pie in the Sky led to a job at the Senator Restaurant, Toronto's oldest restaurant, which is still serving up classic comfort food at Yonge and Dundas.

Meanwhile, my husband at the time, Marcus, who is from Trinidad, got the bug to return to his homeland. We eventually settled on Tobago, Trinidad's sister island, where we'd spend the winters, returning in summer to the Toronto Islands. In the Caribbean, I learned how to bake seasonally with new ingredients such as the baby pineapples that grew in our hedge or the dry coconuts that I used in sweet breads and coconut cream pie.

The people and culture took hold of me. I'd bike to work at a local catering business, a forty-five-minute scenic journey past fragrant Lady of the Night flowers and crystal-blue water; two dogs would happily chase me on my final climb to work. At work, we'd bake, listen to music and trade recipes for coconut bake, rum punch and roti. The Caribbean still flavours my baking to this day—you'll taste it in my lamb patties (page 172) and my famous rum-soaked fruit cake (page 159).

After a decade of spending all or part of each year amid the palm trees and tropical breezes, it was time to return to Canada. But I couldn't bear the cold winters any more. So in May 2002 we landed on warm and sunny Salt Spring, another island with a welcoming community—and all of them, it seemed, loved a good piece of pie.

Salt Spring Island is one of the Southern Gulf Islands between the British Columbia mainland and Vancouver Island. It's a close community of farmers, artisans and escapees from the big city. Surrounded by the pristine waters of the Salish Sea and swept by warm, gentle breezes, Salt Spring is a garden just bursting with bounty. We're fortunate enough to have a wonderful microclimate for growing a bounty of produce: flowers, herbs, berries, pumpkins, vegetables and tree fruits, including hundreds of varieties of apples. (Many heritage ones grow in century-old orchards.) You can even find kiwi fruit and bananas here! No wonder they call this Canada's banana belt. There are plenty of farms on the island, not only for growing produce, but for raising beef cattle, chickens for eggs, goats for cheese and the world-famous Salt Spring lamb. Almost everyone grows something edible in their gardens, and throughout the summer, people will beg me to take their extra rhubarb, raspberries, tomatoes and zucchinis, which grow like crazy here. Come September, I make a variety of chutneys when local growers come to me with squashes and green tomatoes.

We opened Jana's Bake Shop soon after we moved to the island, and we quickly built a loyal following. Since then, there've been significant changes: the bake shop has moved a few times (it's now in its fourth location), my son Kyle is all grown up now and working as a chef in Montreal, and I've remarried to a wonderful man named Lane Grommé—and I can't imagine running Jana's Bake Shop without him. However, other things remain the same: I still make many of my mom's favourite recipes, using as many local, organic ingredients as possible, and we continue to receive kudos all around for our quality.

We're best known for our pies, with their perfectly flaky crust and sweet, but not too sweet, fruit fillings. The wonderfully chewy chocolate-chip-studded cookies (page 43) and the butter tart (page 105)—with its luxurious inch-and-a-half of filling that is neither too dry nor too drippy—are also very popular. Then again, you can't have a big celebration on the island without one of Jana's cakes! In any case, you'll find our pies and cakes at most island fundraisers and parties, as well as places like Moby's Pub, Café Talia and the Salt Spring Inn. And those are our mini-muffins you'll taste as you're waiting for Salt Spring Air to take you over to Vancouver. (And by the way, I like to use the old-school baby muffin tins, which have waffle bottoms and make sixteen, rather than the modern twelve.)

All these years later, I still have the same passion for baking. I don't ring a school bell any more when my butter tarts are ready, but I still live on an island, I still ride my bike and I still bake treats that always sell out. Instead of a cart, though, I have a bake shop, a cozy spot filled with sweet aromas, happy people and, every once in a while, the joyful music of the Caribbean Islands. It's a long way from the Toronto Islands, but Salt Spring is home now.

ESSENTIAL EQUIPMENT

TO MEASURE

- Candy thermometer
- Ice cream scoops for portioning (we prefer Vollrath's 2-oz scoops)
- Measuring cups, dry and liquid
- Measuring spoons
- Ruler
- Scale

TO CUT, BLEND, MASH, POUR AND SCRAPE

- Bench scraper
- Box grater
- Doughnut cutter
- Food processor
- Funnel
- KNIVES:
  Bread knife
  Chef's knife
  Palette knife or offset spatula
  Paring knife
- Pastry blender
- Pastry wheel
- Potato masher

TO MIX

- Assortment of bowls
- Heatproof spatula
- Stand mixer and/or handheld electric mixer
- Whisk
- Wooden spoon

TO BAKE AND COOK

- 6-, 9- and 10-inch round baking pans
- 8-inch square baking pan
- 9 × 13-inch baking pan
- 10-inch springform pan
- Baking sheets
- Canning pot or canner
- Muffin tins
- Parchment paper
- Pie plates
- Pizza tray
- Pyrex or ceramic baking dishes
- Saucepans (small, medium, large)
- Stockpot
- Tart pans
- Tube pans

RECIPE NOTES

Brown sugar is golden;

Butter is unsalted;

Buttermilk, sour cream and
yogurt are full fat;

Corn syrup is golden;

Eggs are large;

Juice is fresh and strained;

Milk is whole;

Molasses is fancy;

Pepper is freshly ground;

Rolled oats *aren't* quick-cooking;

Salt is kosher (unless sea salt is specified);

Sugar is granulated.

In British Columbia, whipping cream can
range between 33% and 36% fat. For my recipes
I use 36%, but both are acceptable options.

BAKING TIPS

BAKING IS AT ONCE art and science. Decorating a cake is art. Combining the right amount of the right ingredients to get a lofty rise and a moist crumb, well, that's science. And that means there are rules to follow, especially if you want to get the best results. Here are some of the things I've learned, to help make your own bakes better.

HOW TO GET THE MOST OUT OF THIS BOOK

Prepare yourself. Even before you turn the oven on, read the recipe through. Compile an ingredients list from the recipe before shopping, which helps to ensure that you have all the ingredients on hand—you don't want to stop in the midst of making a cake to rush out for more milk, or to realize a recipe required advance preparation.

Be organized. I call it the organizational flow: if you're organized, the flow will come. Assemble your tools and measure your ingredients before you start. If eggs, butter and milk need to be at room temperature, take them out ahead of time. Prep your baking pans first and ensure you have the ones suited to your recipe.

Measure carefully. Invest in a good set of measuring cups and spoons. Always use dry measuring cups for dry ingredients and liquid for liquid. When measuring flour, my rule is to fluff, fill and level. A measuring cup dipped into flour will give you a heavier weight, throwing your recipe out of balance. I fluff the flour by hand, then use a scoop or spoon to fill the measuring cup. And be sure to level dry ingredients with a spatula— you'd be surprised how far off a measurement can be if you don't.

Get to know your oven. Pay attention to the temperature setting and time of your bake. Ovens often vary 25 degrees either way. If your cake peaks and cracks, likely your oven is too hot, so next time you'll know to drop the temperature. Also, be sure to turn your oven on to preheat at least 15 minutes prior to baking.

I start most of my bakes on the bottom rack, then move them to the centre rack. If you introduce top heat first, it can flatten cookies and seal the top of cakes and muffins, resulting in a sort of volcanic action when the batter needs somewhere to go. If the heat starts from below, it prevents soggy bottoms on pies and cakes from cracking. It also gives cookies and muffins a nice lift.

UNDER, OVER, INSIDE: BASIC RECIPES

IF YOU BREAK a dessert down into its components, a foundation, a filling and a topping are the essentials that go into so many of our favourite recipes. Mastering these basics opens your world to the creative process of baking, and I guarantee that you'll use them repeatedly in all their varied forms, both in this book and beyond.

UNDER

These are the recipes that form the foundation of your bakes: the flaky crust that will be topped with fruit in a pie, the buttery shell for a creamy tart filling, the crumbly base for a gloriously gooey square.

PIE PASTRY

This pie pastry originally came from my mom, but I have tweaked it over the years so that it's versatile enough for sweet fruit pies, savoury pot pies (pages 178 and 180) and, of course, butter tarts (page 105). A lot of people find pie crust challenging, but trust me, this one is a snap and it works beautifully every time. What makes it so successful is the shortening, which results in a light, flaky pastry crust, and it is forgiving in that you can re-roll your pastry cut-offs and still achieve lovely results (see also Butter vs. Shortening, page 21).

In a small bowl, whisk sugar, vinegar, egg and salt. Pour into a 2-cup liquid measuring cup and add water until measurement is 1 cup exactly. Refrigerate for at least 10 minutes.

Meanwhile, place flour in a large bowl and, using a pastry blender, cut shortening into flour until it is pea sized.

Make a well in the centre of the flour mixture. Pour in the liquid. With quick strokes, and using a pastry scraper or your hands, bring flour from the sides of the bowl into the centre and cover the liquid. Repeat, then fold entire mass over and onto itself, until the liquid has been evenly incorporated. The dough mass should feel "satiny" and consistent.

Divide pastry evenly into 4 pieces. Shape and flatten into disks, wrap in plastic wrap and chill for at least 30 minutes. Alternatively, wrap it, seal in a zip-top freezer bag and freeze for up to 3 months. When ready to use, simply defrost for 1 hour.

Makes 4 (10-inch) pie shells, 2 covered pies or 10–12 pot pies

2 Tbsp packed brown sugar

2 Tbsp cider vinegar

1 egg

2 tsp sea salt

Cold water, as needed

5 cups unbleached all-purpose flour

2 cups vegetable shortening

BUTTERY PASTRY

I use this pastry primarily for rustic tarts like the open-face ones known as galettes. It has a beautiful flaky texture and buttery flavour with just a touch of sweetness. It's a little bit finicky to prepare, but with practice, the result will be well worth the effort.

In a large bowl, whisk flour, sugar and salt. Using a pastry blender, cut butter into flour until it is pea sized, leaving some larger pieces.

Sprinkle water over the flour mixture. Using your hands, quickly distribute the water throughout.

Fold a damp towel underneath the bowl to anchor it. With hands on either side of the dough mass, push the dough forward with the heel of your hand and then bring it back onto itself, working until the dough comes together in one mass.

Place the dough on a lightly floured counter. Press the dough piece to flatten. Fold in half, then in half again. Press again gently with hands, wrap in plastic wrap and chill for 30 minutes. (Alternatively, wrap it, seal in a zip-top freezer bag and freeze for up to 3 months. When ready to use, simply defrost for 3 hours.)

When you're ready to make your tarts, remove pastry from fridge and set aside for 10–15 minutes to allow for easier rolling. Lightly dust a counter and roll pastry into a 10-inch circle, ¼ inch thick, for a large tart (or divide and roll it as needed for your recipe).

Makes 1 (10-inch) free-form tart or 6–8 small rustic tarts

3 cups unbleached all-purpose flour

½ cup sugar

½ tsp salt

1½ cups (3 sticks) cold butter, cut into cubes

¼ cup cold water

Whole-wheat flour, for dusting (see Note)

DUSTING

When I'm making pies and tarts, I always use whole-wheat flour for dusting. The tradition began years ago with Margaret Coleman, a long-time community baker on Ward's Island, who was a very creative cook. It gives the finished pastry a rich colour. And don't be shy—my pastries still come out light and flaky.

BUTTER VS. SHORTENING

PASTRY IS BASICALLY FLOUR + FAT + WATER.

You can use butter, shortening, lard or even oil as the fat, but beware that not every fat works the same way, and some are better for certain applications than others. Fat's role is not just to add flavour, but to keep the layers of flour and water separated as the pie or tart bakes: in general, the longer fat stays solid, the more flakes it will form and the flakier the crust should be. For that reason, you should take care not to overmix your dough.

Butter is the best-tasting fat, but it *can* be a bit finicky—it has a low melting point, so if it's too warm, it can give you a tough pie crust; too cold and it's difficult to roll. If the pieces are too big, they can melt and run out of your crust. It's also hard to re-roll butter pastry dough if you need to. So I don't usually use butter for pie crust, but if you choose to use it for its irreplaceable flavour, you can still get great results if you're patient. And butter is ideal for the sandy-textured tart crust known as *sablé* or *pâte sucrée*, as well as for galettes (page 138) and streusel pastry (page 22).

Vegetable shortening, on the other hand, is a solid fat made from vegetable oil. It has a higher melting point than butter so it's easy to roll and will hold its shape better when baking, making it ideal for pretty fluted edges and decorative details. It also gives you a great, flaky crust. It doesn't have the flavour of butter, though, so it's best for traditional pie crusts. Lard also makes exceptional pastry, but it's essential to use high-quality rendered beef or pork fat, which can be difficult to find. Oil can technically be used—and some people swear by it—but it can give you an unpleasantly mealy texture.

SHORT CRUST PASTRY

This simple, classic butter pastry is used for tarts such as the Double Lemon Tart (page 135). It is traditionally "blind baked" (see Note, page 131), which means baking it without the filling.

In a large bowl, cream butter and icing sugar until smooth. Add flour and salt and stir until just combined.

With floured fingers, press crust evenly into the bottom and up the sides of a fluted tart pan, dusting hands with more flour if they get sticky. Freeze shell for at least 15 minutes before baking.

Makes 1 (10-inch) tart shell

¾ cup (1½ sticks) butter, room temperature

⅓ cup sifted icing sugar

2 cups unbleached all-purpose flour, plus extra for dusting

¼ tsp salt

STREUSEL PASTRY

This cakey, fuller pastry is incredibly easy to make because it requires no pre-baking: you just press it into your baking pan. Streusel pastry works well when baked with freshly sliced apples and topped with vanilla crumble (page 29), but I also like to use it for the base of cheesecake (page 165).

In a medium bowl, cream butter and sugar until smooth. Add eggs, lemon zest and nutmeg and beat into the mixture.

In a large bowl, whisk flour, baking powder and salt. Make a well in the centre, pour in the egg mixture and stir until the dough comes together.

Press the dough into the desired baking pan, making sure to press it halfway up the sides. Then even out the dough in the base of the pan. Chill for 30 minutes before filling and baking. Alternatively, wrap well and freeze for up to 1 month.

Makes 1 (10-inch) cake or tart

¾ cup (1½ sticks) butter, room temperature

¾ cup sugar

2 eggs

1 Tbsp finely grated lemon zest

½ tsp ground nutmeg

3 cups unbleached all-purpose flour

1 Tbsp baking powder

½ tsp salt

PATTY PASTRY

Makes 10–12 (6-inch) patties

½ cup cold water

1 egg

4 cups unbleached
  all-purpose flour

½ tsp turmeric powder

2 tsp sea salt

2 cups vegetable
  shortening

For the best part of a decade, I lived on Tobago, the sister island to Trinidad. I was inspired by the warmth of the people, the music and, of course, the food, which is flavoured by the many cultures who have inhabited these islands. I used to make Jamaican-style patties with a curried chicken filling, but now that I'm on Salt Spring, I use the renowned local lamb instead. The pastry has a shorter consistency than pie pastry because the shortening is worked in longer, and it has a good body to support the meaty filling. As for that unique golden colour, it comes from turmeric, the spice that gives curries their vibrant ochre hue.

In a small bowl or measuring cup, whisk water and egg together. Chill for at least 10 minutes.

Meanwhile, in a large bowl, whisk flour, turmeric and salt. Using a pastry blender, cut shortening into flour until pea sized. Make a well in the centre and pour in the egg mixture.

Using a pastry scraper, quickly and thoroughly incorporate the liquid, starting from the outside in. Flatten the dough into disks, wrap in plastic wrap and chill for 20–30 minutes to relax the dough. Alternatively, wrap it, seal in a zip-top freezer bag and freeze for up to 3 months. When ready to use, simply defrost for 1 hour.

MAKE IT GLUTEN-FREE

GLUTEN-FREE FLOUR BLEND

I decided right away that if I was going to serve gluten-free baking, I wanted to use quality products all the way. I experimented with several flour blends and finally settled on this recipe, which can be used successfully in recipes that call for regular wheat flour. Since gluten-free flour soaks up liquid more than ordinary flour, simply reduce the amount of gluten-free flour in your recipe by two table-spoons for every cup of flour called for.

In a large bowl, whisk all ingredients to combine. Store until ready to use.

Makes 6 cups

2 cups brown rice flour
2 cups coconut flour
2 cups gluten-free oat flour
2 Tbsp guar gum (see Note)

GUAR GUM

Guar gum, also known as guaran, is a common additive in many processed foods. Made from guar beans, it is low in calories and high in fibre, and it is used in gluten-free baked goods to attract water, bind, thicken and emulsify—other-wise, they'd fall apart into dry, disappointing crumbs. Guar gum is typically sold as a powder at specialty grocers or whole food stores.

Frostings, glazes and crumbles add more than just the finishing touches to your cakes, muffins and loaves. They take a bake from fine to fabulous and allow a baker to express their own unique personality. They also introduce versatility to your kitchen: a simple white cake, for instance, can become a whole new experience depending on its topping.

CREAM CHEESE FROSTING

Cream cheese frosting is essential for carrot cake (page 142), but it is also lovely on buttermilk-spice cake (page 143) or chunky apple cake (page 150). The buttercream base gives it the body you need and the cream cheese gives it a nice, tangy flavour; together, they make a luxuriously smooth icing to work with. Just remember to cream the cheese until it's smooth before adding softened buttercream.

In the bowl of a stand mixer fitted with a paddle attachment, blend cream cheese until smooth. Add buttercream and lemon or orange zest and mix well. Scrape down bowl to ensure the ingredients are evenly incorporated. Do not overbeat.

Frosts 1 (9-inch) 2-layer cake, inside and out

1 cup cream cheese, room temperature

2½ cups Buttercream (page 30), room temperature

1–2 Tbsp finely grated lemon or orange zest

SALTED CARAMEL SAUCE

Makes enough to glaze
1 (10-inch) cake

1 cup whipping (36%) cream
¾ cup sugar
Pinch of sea salt

The first time I tasted Salt Spring sea salt, I knew I'd have to bake with it. Philippe Marill harvests the salt from our pristine waters by evaporating it and filters out any impurities, leaving behind perfect flakes and crystals. Of course, you can use any sea salt you prefer. It's perfect in this sauce, which can be used as a topping on a banana cake (page 148), as a glaze on chunky apple cake (page 150) or served alongside gingerbread loaf (page 89). You could even add it to the buttercream for a caramel frosting (page 31). My friend Jackie says I should bottle it and sell it. Maybe one day . . .

In a small saucepan over low heat, heat cream until warm. Turn heat off and leave on stove.

Pour sugar into a wide, deep-sided frying pan and heat over low heat. Swirl the pan until sugar is amber in colour.

Slowly pour warm cream into melted sugar, stirring until the caramel is smooth. (Be careful as it may spatter.) Remove from heat and continue to stir until it has a pouring consistency. Stir in the salt while the caramel is still warm.

LEMON SYRUP

Makes 2 cups

1 cup sugar, plus extra to
    taste
1 cup water
¾ cup fresh lemon juice,
    plus extra to taste
3 whole cloves
1 cinnamon stick
Small slice of fresh ginger

We use this syrup to dip our lemon–poppy seed muffins (page 86), pour it over gingerbread loaf (page 89) and brush it over pound cake (page 145). You could even use it in cocktails, if you wanted to. In fact, that's a great idea. Store it in a sterilized glass jar, and it will keep in the fridge for 2 weeks.

Combine ingredients in a medium saucepan and cook over low heat, stirring constantly, until sugar dissolves. Cook for another minute. Taste and adjust flavour with more sugar or lemon juice for a sweet, citrusy balance. Cool to room temperature, then strain. Store in a glass jar in the fridge for up to 2 weeks.

PUMPKIN GLAZE

In the days when my mom and I were wheeling the pastry cart around the Toronto Islands, I used to serve pumpkin doughnuts (page 100)—they were such a huge hit that I promised myself they'd be in this book. This glaze has a beautiful shine for a classic doughnut look and can also be poured over a cake, loaf or cupcakes.

In a medium bowl, combine pumpkin purée, corn syrup and vanilla and mix well. Stir in icing sugar and pumpkin pie spice. Pour in hot water and whisk until smooth. Use immediately.

Makes enough to glaze 24 (3-inch) doughnuts

¼ cup store-bought or homemade pumpkin purée (page 36)

1 Tbsp corn syrup

½ tsp vanilla extract

2 cups sifted icing sugar

½ tsp pumpkin pie spice

¼ cup hot water

OATMEAL CRUMBLE

If you don't want to make a top for your pie, you can use this as an alternative—this super-versatile crumble is easy to make and functions similarly to a crisp topping. It's perfect for adding wonderful texture to treats such as cranberry-orange crumble muffins (page 85) or apple crisp (page 108).

In a large bowl, whisk dry ingredients together to combine. Add butter and use your hands to incorporate until the mixture is crumbly.

Makes enough to top 3 (10-inch) pies or 12 muffins or tarts

3 cups rolled oats

1½ cups packed brown sugar

1½ cups unbleached all-purpose flour

1½ tsp baking powder

1½ tsp ground cinnamon

1 tsp salt

¾ cup (1½ sticks) butter, room temperature

TO FREEZE
Keep ready-prepped crumble topping for occasions when you need a quick dessert fix. Simply store the mixture in a freezer-proof airtight container or zip-top freezer bag for up to 3 months.

CINNAMON CRUMBLE

*Makes enough to cover
3 (10-inch) pies or 2 fruit
crisps*

2 cups unbleached
    all-purpose flour
1½ cups packed brown
    sugar
1 tsp baking powder
1 Tbsp ground cinnamon
½ tsp salt
1½ cups (3 sticks) butter,
    room temperature

I love using this on top of muffins, fruit pies and even fruit squares. It's a great topping for crisps and cobblers because it bakes up a little crisper than a traditional oatmeal crumble.

In a large bowl, whisk dry ingredients together to combine. Add butter and use your hands to incorporate until the mixture is crumbly.

See Note below on how to freeze.

VANILLA CRUMBLE

*Makes enough for
1 (9 × 13-inch) pan of squares*

½ cup (1 stick) butter,
    melted
½ cup sugar
1 tsp vanilla extract
1½ cups unbleached
    all-purpose flour
¼ tsp salt

This is another great topping for fruit custard squares. It can be used just like any of the other crumble toppings, but has the added fragrance of sweet, seductive vanilla.

In a large bowl, combine butter, sugar and vanilla. Stir in flour and salt and combine until the mixture is crumbly.

TO FREEZE

Keep ready-prepped crumble topping for occasions when you need a quick dessert fix. Simply store the mixture in a freezer-proof airtight container or zip-top freezer bag for up to 3 months.

BUTTERCREAM

FROSTS I (IO-INCH) 2-LAYER CAKE, INSIDE AND OUT

This versatile recipe is the base for all of my favourite frostings. It's beautifully spreadable and consistent, thanks in part to a secret ingredient: shortening, which keeps the texture creamy and stops the buttercream from curdling.

¼ cup sugar

2 eggs

Pinch of sea salt

1¼ cups (2½ sticks) butter, room temperature, cut into 1-inch chunks

¼ cup vegetable shortening

3 cups sifted icing sugar

2 tsp vanilla extract

Fill a medium saucepan a quarter full with water and bring to a simmer over medium-low heat.

In a small heatproof bowl, whisk sugar, eggs and salt. Place the bowl over the simmering water and whisk continuously. If the water comes to a boil or begins to steam, turn off heat. Whisk until the mixture reaches 120°F, or until hot to the touch and thick enough to coat the back of a spoon.

Pour the egg mixture into the bowl of a stand mixer fitted with a paddle attachment and beat until it is thick and pale. (Alternatively, use a whisk and heatproof spatula to mix by hand.) With the mixer running, add butter and shortening a little at a time and beat until light and fluffy. Turn mixer off, remove bowl from mixer and scrape down to ensure the ingredients are evenly incorporated.

Return bowl to mixer and, on low speed, slowly add icing sugar and vanilla and mix until incorporated. Increase speed and beat until light and fluffy. Remove bowl from mixer, scrape down again and beat for another 2 minutes. Use immediately. (Alternatively, store in the fridge for up to 2 weeks. When ready to use, allow buttercream to soften at room temperature and beat until smooth and spreadable.)

BUTTERCREAM FLAVOURS

Here are just a few of my favourites, and they're super-easy to make. I simply add the ingredient to the finished frosting and *voilà*! If you like a specific flavour, then I encourage you to experiment. Maybe a rounded mocha, a nutty matcha or a fragrant orange blossom? You'll soon discover that the possibilities are endless.

1 LEMON
1 cup Lemon Curd (page 34)

2 CARAMEL
1 cup Salted Caramel Sauce (page 27)

3 PEANUT BUTTER
½–1 cup natural creamy peanut butter

4 CHOCOLATE
1½ cups room-temperature Ganache (page 37)

PEANUT BUTTER
BUTTERCREAM
(page 31)

BASIC
BUTTERCREAM
(page 30)

LEMON CURD
(page 34)

SALTED CARAMEL SAUCE
(page 27)

GANACHE
(page 37)

Between the base and the topping comes the substance of your baked goods: the filling. Ganaches, compotes and custards, whether savoury or sweet, form the essence of pies, cakes, tarts, quiches and so much more.

LEMON CURD

Use this lovely, lemony custard as a filling in tarts, cakes and squares. Mix a cup of it with buttercream (page 30) for a bright, sunshiny frosting. Serve it as a sauce or use it as a spread on toast. You might even be tempted to eat it with a spoon straight from the jar, it's that good. Unlike many recipes, this one calls for both whole eggs and egg yolks, so you won't have quite as many leftover egg whites to deal with. Just be sure to follow the steps in the right order, paying attention to timing and temperature, so you get the consistency you want.

Makes 2 cups

2 eggs
2 egg yolks
½ cup (1 stick) butter
1 cup sugar
½ cup fresh lemon juice
1 Tbsp finely grated lemon zest

In a small bowl, whisk whole eggs and yolks together. Set aside.

Heat butter in a medium saucepan set over low heat. When butter is almost melted, whisk in sugar, eggs and lemon juice. Using a heatproof spatula, stir continuously until the mixture thickens and coats the back of a spoon. Do not allow the curd to boil.

Place lemon zest in a glass or steel bowl. Strain lemon curd into the bowl, pressing lightly on it but taking care to strain out any solids. Stir to incorporate lemon zest. Set aside to cool slightly, then cover with plastic wrap and refrigerate for at least 2 hours, but preferably overnight.

VANILLA CUSTARD

Makes 3 cups

2 cups light (10%) cream

3 egg yolks, room temperature

⅓ cup sugar

3 Tbsp cornstarch

Pinch of sea salt

1 Tbsp butter

2 tsp vanilla extract

One of my best memories from when I was a little girl is my mom's applesauce custard cake in a bowl—a simple cake served with homemade applesauce and warm custard. A dessert just couldn't get any better. Based on that memory, I have made my own adaptation of vanilla custard. Pour custard while still warm over a slice of gingerbread loaf (page 89) or apple crisp (page 108).

In a medium saucepan, warm cream until hot. Turn off heat and leave cream on the stove.

In a large bowl, whisk egg yolks, sugar, cornstarch and salt until thick and pale.

Place a damp towel under the bowl to anchor. Slowly pour the hot cream into the egg mixture, a little at a time, whisking until fully incorporated.

Pour the mixture into a clean saucepan and set over medium heat. Stir with a whisk, then change to a heatproof spatula. (The spatula helps to get into crevices where the custard tends to settle.) Stir until custard is smooth and thickened and has just come to a boil, or when it reaches a temperature of 175°F.

Remove from heat and stir in butter and vanilla. Pour into a glass or stainless bowl. Serve warm, or cover cooled custard with plastic wrap and chill.

TEMPERING EGGS

When you add hot liquid to eggs, you have a recipe for scrambled or curdled eggs, which is not what you want in your rich, velvety custard. The key here is to temper your eggs, which simply means slowly bringing them up to heat. The way to do this is by adding a very little bit of hot liquid at a time, whisking it in thoroughly, then adding a bit more, and repeating until all the liquid has been incorporated. A surefire way to prevent your custard from scrambling is to remove it from the heat the second it reaches 175°F on an instant-read thermometer, then place the bowl in an ice bath and keep whisking until it cools to room temperature. If you need to chill it, place a sheet of plastic wrap right on the surface of the custard to prevent a skin from forming.

PUMPKIN PURÉE

You can, of course, use purchased unsweetened pumpkin purée, but here on the island, I like to make my own from the sugar pumpkins grown at Bon Acres Farm—they have the sweetest, most pumpkin-y flavour. If you do make your own, be sure to do so a day in advance so it has time to drain overnight.

1 sugar pumpkin, cut in half, seeded and stringy fibres removed

Preheat the oven to 350°F.

Put pumpkin on a baking sheet, flesh-side down, and roast for 1 hour. Set aside to cool, then scrape out the flesh into a bowl and mash it until completely smooth. As the flesh contains a lot of water, put the purée into a colander set over a bowl and let it drain overnight in the fridge. (You'll have a richer texture and more intense flavour as a result.)

FRUIT COMPOTE

This compote is designed to go under a cheesecake (page 165), but there's no stopping you from adding it to fruit tarts (page 138) or using it as an accompaniment for a simple pound cake (page 145) or other desserts. You can make it with any kind of fruit—great choices include plums, rhubarb, berries or sour cherries. I tend to use what's in season, although you could certainly use frozen fruit instead. No need to thaw—the juices will release as you make the compote.

Makes enough for 1 (10-inch) cheesecake or 12 rustic tarts

5 cups fruit, pitted and chopped into ½-inch pieces, if necessary

1¼ cups sugar

Finely grated zest and juice of 1 lemon

1 tsp freshly grated ginger (optional)

¼ cup cornstarch

In a medium saucepan over low heat, combine fruit, sugar, lemon juice and zest and ginger (if using). Stir until sugar has melted and juices are released. Strain liquid into a small bowl and set aside to cool. Once cooled, add cornstarch to the bowl and mix well.

Meanwhile, return the fruit back to the saucepan and heat over low heat. Pour the cornstarch mixture into the saucepan and stir continuously, until the mixture just comes to a boil. Once the compote is clear and thick, remove from heat. Pour into a glass or stainless-steel bowl to cool. Use as needed or cover with plastic wrap and refrigerate.

GANACHE

Makes 2 cups

1 cup whipping (36%) cream

1 cinnamon stick

10 oz semi-sweet baking chocolate, chopped (about 2 cups)

Ganache sounds fancy and intimidating, right? But ganache is easy to make if you have the right ingredients. And it's so versatile you'll want to make it again and again—you can use it to ice a cake or in truffles, tarts, coconut macaroons and even buttercream (page 30). Use a good-quality baking chocolate, which is designed to melt, and be sure to chop it in small, equal-sized pieces.

In a medium saucepan set over low heat, combine cream and cinnamon stick and cook until hot. (Do not allow cream to boil.) Turn off heat and discard cinnamon stick.

Add chocolate and stir until melted and smooth. Cool ganache to room temperature, then use as needed.

CHOCOLATE

All chocolate may be delicious, but not all chocolate is made to work the same way in baking. Some chocolate, such as chocolate chips, is manufactured to keep its shape, and is meant for cookies and loaves. But if you want to make a ganache for a topping or filling, you need a chocolate that is designed to melt, and that means a baking or couverture chocolate, which has a higher amount of cocoa butter. (The more cocoa butter, the more fluid it will be when it melts.)

The amount of cacao contained in the chocolate also makes a difference: milk chocolate usually has the least and can be quite sweet and bland; unsweetened and bittersweet dark chocolate can be quite bitter indeed. My favourite chocolate to use for ganache is a 60% to 70% cacao semi-sweet dark chocolate, which is bold, fruity and well balanced. Guittard, Callebaut and Ghirardelli are good options.

COOKIES

WHO DOESN'T LOVE cookies? They're sweet little bites of bliss that you can simply grab and go. They're also the easiest things to bake, which is great news, since they're among the most popular treats you can offer. I know, because at the bake shop, our cookies just fly off the shelves, whether they're the hearty hermit cookies (page 41), the lunchbox-worthy chocolate chippers (page 43) or the elegant espresso cookies (page 53) that are so perfect for afternoon coffee breaks. Turn the page to find your own Cookie Monster's favourite.

Also, be sure to give your cookies room to grow. The way I was taught, when you place cookies on a baking sheet, every other row should have an even number—for example, three, two, three, two and so on—giving each cookie enough space to spread without touching its neighbours.

These could be my favourite cookies of all, and they're one
of the most popular with our customers, too. They're soft,
chewy and bursting with ginger flavour. If you prefer a crispier cookie,
you could prepare them as you would an icebox cookie:
simply put the dough on wax paper, shape the dough into a log,
then chill for 30 minutes. When ready, simply slice and bake.
You can also put a piece of crystallized ginger on top of each
cookie partway through baking for an even spicier flavour.

GINGER COOKIES

MAKES 24–36 COOKIES

Preheat the oven to 350°F. Line a baking sheet with parchment paper.

In a bowl, whisk flour, baking soda, spices and salt.

In the bowl of a stand mixer fitted with a paddle attachment, cream butter, sugars and lemon zest until smooth. Beat in eggs and molasses. Stir in the flour mixture and blend until batter is smooth.

Using an ice cream scoop, scoop cookies onto the prepared baking sheet, evenly spacing them 2 inches apart. Bake on the bottom rack for 10 minutes. Remove from oven, then press the back of a spoon into the centres of the half-baked cookies. Bake cookies on the centre rack for another 7–10 minutes, until the cookies are lightly golden. Remove from oven and set aside to cool.

5½ cups unbleached
  all-purpose flour

4 tsp baking soda

1 Tbsp ground ginger

4 tsp ground cinnamon

2 tsp salt

1½ cups (3 sticks) butter,
  room temperature

2 cups packed brown sugar

2 cups sugar

1 Tbsp finely grated lemon
  zest

2 eggs

1 cup fancy molasses

TO FREEZE

Place the dough on a large piece of wax paper, shape and roll the dough into a log, then wrap it up and freeze until solid. Transfer to a zip-top freezer bag and freeze for up to 3 months. When ready to serve, defrost for 7–10 minutes, then slice. Bake from frozen as per instructions.

Although no one is sure where the name originated,
these cookies date back to at least the 1870s, when they were
prized for their taste as well as their long-lasting freshness
(making them ideal for picnics and school lunches).
They're spicy and loaded with nuts and fruit, with a
rounded shape and an interesting texture that is neither
crispy nor soft and chewy—it's just irresistible.

HERMIT COOKIES

MAKES 24 COOKIES

2¾ cups unbleached
all-purpose flour

1½ tsp ground cinnamon

1 tsp ground allspice

½ tsp ground nutmeg

1 tsp baking soda

1 tsp salt

1 cup (2 sticks) butter, room
temperature

1½ cups packed brown
sugar

2 eggs

⅓ cup cold coffee

1 cup chopped walnuts

1 cup raisins

2 cups coarsely chopped
dried apricots

Preheat the oven to 350°F. Line a baking sheet with parchment paper.

In a bowl, whisk flour, spices, baking soda and salt.

In the bowl of a stand mixer fitted with a paddle attachment, cream butter and sugar until smooth. Beat in eggs, then add coffee and mix well. Stir in the flour mixture, followed by walnuts, raisins and apricots, and mix well.

Using an ice cream scoop, scoop cookies onto the prepared baking sheet, evenly spacing them 2 inches apart. Bake on the bottom rack for 7–10 minutes. Move the baking sheet to the centre rack and bake for another 7–10 minutes, until the cookies are lightly golden. Remove from oven and set aside to cool.

TO FREEZE

Portion the dough on a baking sheet as if you were about to bake the cookies and freeze it. Once frozen, transfer to a zip-top freezer bag and store in the freezer for up to 3 months. When ready to serve, simply bake from frozen as per instructions.

This cookie is meant to retain a chewy texture in the centre and have more crunch towards the edges, for the best of all cookie worlds. It's all in how you bake them. If you start them on the bottom rack of the oven, they get a burst of energy that starts to set the outside of the cookie, making it crisp on the edges. Then we flatten them a little and move them up to the second rack, where they continue to bake. The result? Cookie perfection.

CHOCOLATE CHIPPERS

MAKES 24–36 COOKIES

7½ cups unbleached all-purpose flour

2 tsp salt

2 tsp baking soda

2¼ cups (4½ sticks) butter, room temperature

2½ cups packed brown sugar

1 cup sugar

3 eggs

2 tsp vanilla extract

3 cups chocolate chips

TO FREEZE

Portion the dough on a baking sheet as if you were about to bake the cookies and freeze it. Once frozen, transfer to a zip-top freezer bag and store in the freezer for up to 3 months. When ready to serve, simply bake from frozen as per instructions.

Preheat the oven to 350°F. Line a baking sheet with parchment paper.

In a large bowl, whisk flour, salt and baking soda until combined.

In another large bowl, cream butter and sugars until smooth. Beat in eggs and vanilla.

Pour dry ingredients into the wet mixture and mix well. Stir in chocolate chips until just mixed. Using an ice cream scoop, scoop cookies onto the prepared baking sheet, evenly spacing them 2 inches apart.

Bake on the bottom rack for 7 minutes. Remove from oven, then press the back of a spoon into the centres of the half-baked cookies. Bake cookies on the centre rack for 7 minutes or until cookies have lightly browned edges. Remove from oven and set aside to cool.

The name says it all—you might just become addicted
to these chocolatey morsels. We've been making them since
I opened the bake shop; they're so good and so easy.
You can make it all in a large saucepan: just melt the chocolate and
butter, remove from heat and stir everything in. Simply delicious.

CHOCOLATE-PECAN JUNKIES

MAKES 12–18 COOKIES

Preheat the oven to 350°F. Line a baking sheet with parchment paper.

In a small bowl, whisk sugar and cocoa powder. Set aside.

In a separate bowl, whisk flour, baking powder and salt until combined. Set aside.

Put butter and chocolate into a large saucepan and gently melt over low heat. Remove from heat, add the cocoa mixture and stir until smooth. Beat in eggs, one at a time. Fold in the flour mixture, followed by chocolate chips and pecans. Set aside and cool to room temperature. The batter should be cool enough so that the cookies do not spread, but stay rounded and a little moist in the centre when baked. (If you want a flatter cookie, scoop the cookie dough while the batter is still a little warm and allow room for spreading.)

¾ cup sugar

¼ cup Dutch process cocoa powder, sifted (see Note)

¼ cup unbleached all-purpose flour

½ tsp baking powder

½ tsp sea salt

2 Tbsp butter, room temperature

6 oz semi-sweet baking chocolate, chopped (about 1¼ cups)

2 eggs

1 cup chocolate chips

1 cup chopped pecans

44

Using an ice cream scoop, scoop cookies onto the prepared baking sheet, evenly spacing them 2 inches apart. Bake on the bottom rack for 7 minutes or until the cookies are no longer wet on the bottom. You can test this by carefully lifting a cookie: if it lifts without sticking, it's ready. Move the baking sheet to the centre rack and bake for another 7 minutes, or until cookies lift easily from the paper. Remove from oven and set aside to cool.

DUTCH PROCESS COCOA POWDER

This is also known as alkalized cocoa powder, having been washed with a potassium carbonate solution. It's smoother, darker and milder in flavour.

TO FREEZE

Portion the dough on a baking sheet as if you were about to bake the cookies and freeze it. Once frozen, transfer to a zip-top freezer bag and store in the freezer for up to 3 months. When ready to serve, simply bake from frozen as per instructions.

ICEBOX SHORTBREAD

MAKES 4 ROLLS, ABOUT 30 COOKIES PER ROLL

This shortbread is off-the-charts awesome—if I do say so myself! I make it two ways. The traditional way to make shortbread is to pat the dough into a pan, pre-slice it into bars, dock them (poking them a few times with a fork allows trapped air to escape so that the dough doesn't puff as it bakes), then re-slice after they bake. But I find it's a little easier to make shortbread as you would a traditional icebox cookie. Put the dough on wax paper, roll the dough into a log, then wrap and freeze for at least 30 minutes. When you're ready for them, simply slice and bake as needed.

6 cups unbleached
   all-purpose flour
3 cups cornstarch
2½ cups sifted icing sugar
2 tsp sea salt
4 cups (8 sticks) butter,
   room temperature

Set out 4 large sheets of parchment paper, each 12 × 18 inches.

In a large bowl, whisk flour, cornstarch, icing sugar and salt to combine well. Using your hands, work butter into the mixture, until just combined. Push the dough together and gently knead until the dough is smooth. Divide the dough into 4 equal portions.

Place each portion onto a sheet of parchment paper. Fold bottom half of parchment over the dough to cover and shape into a smooth, uniform log, 2 inches in diameter. Press the dough together as you roll to remove any air pockets. Chill cookie logs in the freezer for 30 minutes or until firm. (To freeze for future use, transfer the wrapped logs to a zip-top freezer bag and freeze for up to 3 months.)

Preheat the oven to 300°F. Line baking sheets with parchment paper.

Remove the cookie dough from the freezer and let it sit at room temperature for 15 minutes, or until soft enough to slice. Cut into ½-inch-thick slices and place cookies onto the prepared baking sheets. Bake on the bottom rack for 10 minutes or until cookies will slide when gently moved. Move the baking sheets to the centre rack and bake for another 10–15 minutes, until cookies have lightly golden edges. Remove from oven and set aside to cool.

SHORT AND SWEET

The flavour combinations for this versatile recipe are only limited by your imagination. Simply mix in the ingredients after kneading the dough, then follow the remaining instructions. Freeze them for later and you'll have delicious, ready-made shortbread for any occasion without having to break a sweat.

1 ORANGE-PECAN
Finely grated zest of 1 orange
2 cups chopped, lightly toasted pecans

2 CRANBERRY-LEMON
Finely grated zest of 1 lemon
2 cups dried cranberries

3 LEMON-POPPY SEED
Finely grated zest of 1 lemon
½ cup poppy seeds

4 ROSEMARY-DRIED APPLE
1 sprig rosemary, finely chopped
2 cups dried apple, coarsely chopped

5 TRINI SHORTBREAD
2 Tbsp rum extract
2 cups unsweetened shredded coconut
1 cup dried pineapple, finely chopped

6 LAVENDER
1 Tbsp organic dried lavender

7 ROSEWATER-PISTACHIO-CARDAMOM
1 tsp rosewater
1 tsp ground cardamom
1 cup shelled pistachios, coarsely chopped

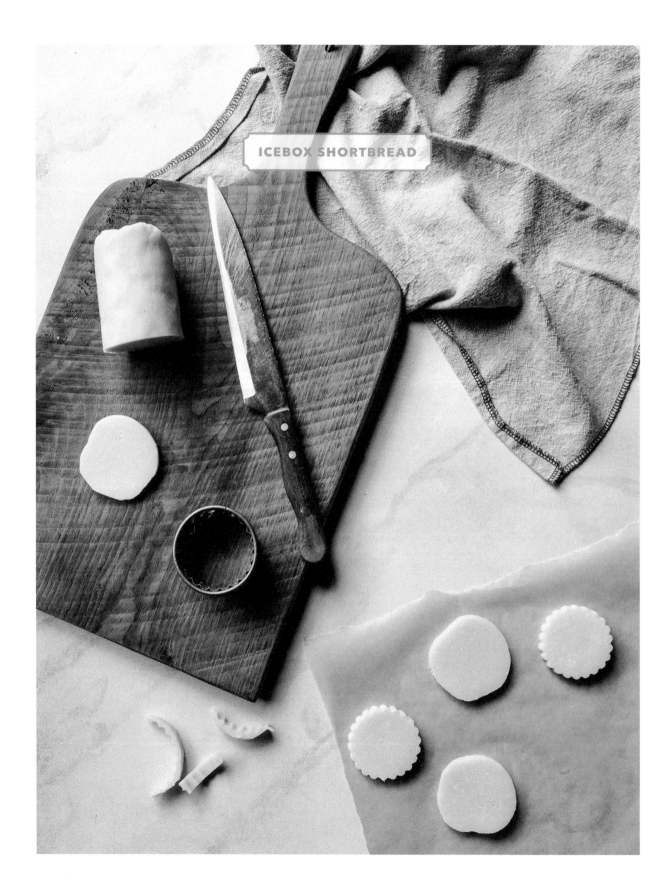

ICEBOX SHORTBREAD

For those who love oatmeal cookies but object to the raisins, these are wonderfully chewy with a soft centre and the bright bite of cranberries. At once wholesome and flavourful, they're always a popular choice.

CHOCOLATE-CRANBERRY-OATMEAL COOKIES

MAKES 24 COOKIES

Preheat the oven to 350°F. Line a baking sheet with parchment paper.

In a small bowl, whisk flour, baking soda and salt.

In the bowl of a stand mixer fitted with a paddle attachment, cream butter and sugar until smooth. Beat in eggs. Stir in orange zest and rolled oats. Stir in the flour mixture, followed by the chocolate chips and cranberries. Blend until batter is smooth and consistent.

Using an ice cream scoop, scoop cookies onto the prepared baking sheet, evenly spacing them 2 inches apart. Bake on the bottom rack for 7 minutes. Remove from oven, then press the back of a spoon into the centres of the half-baked cookies. Bake cookies on the centre rack for another 7–10 minutes, until cookies are lightly golden. Remove from oven and set aside to cool.

3 cups unbleached all-purpose flour

2 tsp baking soda

2 tsp salt

2 cups (4 sticks) butter, room temperature

4 cups packed brown sugar

4 eggs

2 Tbsp finely grated orange zest

7 cups rolled oats

2 cups chocolate chips

2 cups dried cranberries

TO FREEZE

Portion the dough on a baking sheet as if you were about to bake the cookies and freeze it. Once frozen, transfer to a zip-top freezer bag and store in the freezer for up to 3 months. When ready to serve, simply bake from frozen as per instructions.

The chocolate and coconut make for a flavourful update on an old-school classic. For those who like a cookie that crunches but is still delicate, these are the perfect lunchbox treats.

CRISPY COCONUT-CHOCOLATE-OATMEAL COOKIES

MAKES 24 COOKIES

2 cups unbleached all-purpose flour

2 tsp baking powder

½ tsp baking soda

1 tsp sea salt

1½ cups (3 sticks) butter, room temperature

1½ cups packed brown sugar

¾ cup sugar

2 eggs

2 tsp vanilla extract

4 cups rolled oats

1 cup chocolate chips

1 cup unsweetened flaked coconut

Preheat the oven to 350°F. Line a baking sheet with parchment paper.

In a small bowl, whisk flour, baking powder, baking soda and salt.

In the bowl of a stand mixer fitted with a paddle attachment, cream butter and sugars until well blended. Beat in eggs and vanilla. Stir in rolled oats until combined, then add the flour mixture and mix well. Stir in chocolate chips and coconut.

Using an ice cream scoop, scoop cookies onto the prepared baking sheet, evenly spacing them 2 inches apart. Bake on the bottom rack for 7 minutes. Remove from oven, then press the back of a spoon into the centres of the half-baked cookies. Bake cookies on the centre rack for another 7–10 minutes, or until cookies have lightly browned edges. Remove from oven and set aside to cool.

TO FREEZE

Portion the dough on a baking sheet as if you were about to bake the cookies and freeze it. Once frozen, transfer to a zip-top freezer bag and store in the freezer for up to 3 months. When ready to serve, simply bake from frozen as per instructions.

Neither chewy nor crisp, these cookies have a wonderfully buttery, sandy texture and a bold coffee flavour, making them a sophisticated sweet for when that coffee craving hits. Don't be tempted to substitute any other type of coffee for the instant espresso powder—nothing else will give you the easy mixability or the depth of flavour.

CAFÉ ESPRESSO COOKIES

MAKES 18–24 COOKIES

3½ cups unbleached all-purpose flour

¼ cup instant espresso powder

1 tsp baking powder

1 tsp baking soda

½ tsp salt

1½ cups (3 sticks) butter, room temperature

1 cup packed brown sugar

¾ cup sugar

4 egg yolks

Chocolate-covered coffee beans (optional)

Preheat the oven to 350°F. Line a baking sheet with parchment paper.

In a large bowl, whisk flour, espresso powder, baking powder, baking soda and salt.

In the bowl of a stand mixer fitted with a paddle attachment, cream butter and sugars until smooth. Beat in egg yolks. Stir in the flour mixture and mix well until batter is smooth.

Using an ice cream scoop, scoop cookies onto the prepared baking sheet, evenly spacing them 2 inches apart. Flatten to a ½-inch thickness. Press a chocolate-covered coffee bean (if using) into the centre of each cookie. Bake for 15 minutes or until cookies are lightly golden and firm. Remove from oven and set aside to cool.

TO FREEZE

Place the dough on a large piece of wax paper, shape and roll the dough into a log, then wrap it up and freeze until solid. Transfer to a zip-top bag and freeze for up to 3 months. When ready to serve, defrost for 7–10 minutes, then slice. Bake from frozen as per instructions.

For those who love a peanut butter cookie, this is one of the best. We make them big and substantial, with an almost chewy texture and a super-peanutty flavour that isn't too sweet. A perfect pick-me-up for your mid-afternoon coffee or tea break.

PEANUT BUTTER COOKIES

MAKES 24–36 COOKIES

Preheat the oven to 350°F. Line a baking sheet with parchment paper.

In a large bowl, whisk flour, baking soda and salt.

In the bowl of a stand mixer fitted with a paddle attachment, cream peanut butter, butter and sugars until smooth. Beat in eggs and vanilla. Stir in dry ingredients, mixing until batter is smooth. Using an ice cream scoop, scoop cookies onto the prepared baking sheet, evenly spacing them 2 inches apart.

Bake on the bottom rack for 8 minutes. Remove from oven, then use the back of a fork to make hash marks on the cookies. Bake cookies on the centre rack for another 8–10 minutes or until cookies are firm and lightly golden. Remove from oven and set aside to cool.

5¼ cups unbleached all-purpose flour

1 Tbsp baking soda

1 tsp salt

3 cups smooth peanut butter

2 cups (4 sticks) butter, room temperature

1½ cups packed brown sugar

1¼ cups sugar

3 eggs

1 Tbsp vanilla extract

TO FREEZE
Place the dough on a large piece of wax paper, shape and roll the dough into a log, then wrap it up and freeze until solid. Transfer to a zip-top bag and freeze for up to 3 months. When ready to serve, defrost for 7–10 minutes, then slice. Bake from frozen as per instructions.

SLICES AND SQUARES

S LICES AND SQUARES are the perfect in-between treats to satisfy almost any craving. They offer the instant gratification of a cookie, the layered textures that appeal to pie lovers and the slightly more dressed-up, dinner-party-ready appeal of a cake. And yet they are among the easiest things to bake: no fuss, very little mess, all delicious, all the time. See? Perfect.

*I wanted to dedicate something to my mother, Barbara,
and these turned out to be the perfect tribute.
My mother has been a cyclist her whole life, and I knew
she'd love an energy bar to keep those wheels turning.
But I didn't want to make a dry energy bar. This one is chewy,
wholesome and just plain good. It's the perfect snack to
keep my energy up when I'm exploring Salt Spring by bike.*

BARBARS

MAKES 24 BARS

Butter, for greasing

1 cup shelled pumpkin seeds

1 cup shelled sunflower seeds

½ cup sesame seeds

2 cups peanut butter

1 cup honey

¼ cup water

1 Tbsp sea salt

3½ cups rolled oats

2 cups chocolate chips

2 cups dried cranberries

1½ cups unsweetened flaked coconut

1 cup ground flaxseed

Preheat the oven to 300°F. Generously grease a 12 × 18-inch rimmed baking sheet.

In a small bowl, combine pumpkin, sunflower and sesame seeds and mix well. Spread the mixture onto an ungreased baking sheet and toast for 10 minutes, or until fragrant and lightly browned. Remove from oven and allow seeds to cool.

In a large bowl, cream peanut butter, honey, water and salt until smooth. Stir in oats, chocolate chips, cranberries, coconut, flaxseed and toasted seeds and mix well.

Drop batter onto the prepared baking sheet. Spread out, making sure it is evenly distributed, and press firmly into the pan. Bake for 15 minutes or until lightly golden.

Remove from oven and, when cooled, cut into 24 bars or squares.

I've been making these brownies since the beginning,
back in the days of the cart and the school bell.
And the recipe is probably unchanged except that I've
cut back on the sugar. Why mess with perfection?
This old-fashioned, super-chocolatey brownie is a winner.

WALNUT BROWNIES

MAKES 1 (9 × 13-INCH) PAN OF BROWNIES

Preheat the oven to 350°F. Grease a 9 × 13-inch baking pan.
In a large bowl, beat eggs, sugar, vanilla and salt until pale.
Melt butter in a medium saucepan over low heat. Remove
from heat and stir in cocoa powder until smooth.

Add the cocoa mixture to the egg mixture and mix well.
Fold in flour and walnuts and stir until evenly combined.

Pour the batter into the prepared baking pan and bake on
the bottom rack for 20 minutes. Move to the centre rack and
bake for another 15 minutes. Remove from oven and set aside
to cool. Slice, then serve.

1½ cups (3 sticks) butter,
plus extra for greasing

6 eggs

3 cups sugar

2 tsp vanilla extract

1 tsp salt

1½ cups Dutch process
cocoa powder, sifted
(see Note, page 45)

2 cups unbleached
all-purpose flour

2 cups chopped walnuts

Vancouver Island's "Hub City," as Nanaimo is nicknamed, is famous for two things: its annual bathtub races around the harbour, and the sweet treat that is ubiquitous on this coast. It's an unbaked layered bar: a chewy, chocolatey, coconut-and-graham-cracker base, golden custard in the middle, firm chocolate on top. It likely dates to the 1940s and food historians believe that the *Vancouver Sun*'s fictional food columnist Edith Adams named it in the 1950s. In any case, the Nanaimo bar gives the butter tart a run for its money as the unofficial dessert of Canada.

NANAIMO BARS

MAKES 16 BARS

FIRST LAYER
½ cup (1 stick) butter, plus extra for greasing

¼ cup sugar

⅓ cup Dutch process cocoa powder, sifted (see Note, page 45)

1 egg, beaten

1¼ cups graham wafer crumbs

1 cup unsweetened shredded coconut

½ cup finely chopped nuts, such as walnuts, pecans, almonds or filberts

SECOND LAYER
½ cup (1 stick) butter, room temperature

3 Tbsp whipping (36%) cream

3 Tbsp Bird's Instant Custard Powder

2 cups sifted icing sugar

THIRD LAYER
5 oz semi-sweet baking chocolate, chopped (about 1 cup)

2 Tbsp butter

FIRST LAYER Grease an 8-inch baking pan.

Put butter, sugar and cocoa powder into the top of a double boiler and heat over medium heat. Stir until butter has melted and mixture is smooth.

Remove from heat and stir in beaten egg, then stir in crumbs, coconut and nuts. Pour the mixture into the prepared baking pan, spread out evenly and press firmly. Set aside.

SECOND LAYER In a medium bowl, combine ingredients and beat until smooth. Pour the mixture over the base, spreading evenly. Place in fridge and chill until firm.

THIRD LAYER Combine chocolate and butter in a double boiler and heat over medium heat until melted. Pour the chocolate mixture over the chilled custard and spread evenly.

Chill the Nanaimo bars in the fridge until firm. Slice, then serve.

If you love pumpkin pie, you'll adore these squares. They feature a rich, sweetly spiced pumpkin custard on a cinnamon shortbread base; it's a nice marriage of all the flavours, but even better, it's very easy to make.

PUMPKIN-CINNAMON SHORTBREAD SQUARES

MAKES 1 (9 × 13-INCH) PAN OF SQUARES

Preheat the oven to 350°F. Line a 9 × 13-inch baking pan with parchment paper, allowing the paper to come up the sides.

In a large bowl, cream butter, sugar, 3 tsp cinnamon and salt until smooth. Stir in flour and mix until combined. Press the mixture evenly into the bottom of the prepared pan. Chill for 10 minutes.

Bake on the bottom rack of oven for 15 minutes. Move to the centre rack and bake for 10–15 minutes or until golden. Set aside to cool.

Reduce oven temperature to 300°F.

In a large bowl, combine pumpkin purée, condensed milk, eggs, remaining 2 tsp cinnamon and ground ginger and whisk until smooth. Pour filling over baked crust and bake on the centre rack for 15–20 minutes, until custard is just set and no longer jiggly.

Remove from oven and set aside to cool. Slice, then serve.

1 cup (2 sticks) butter, room temperature

¾ cup packed brown sugar

5 tsp ground cinnamon, divided

½ tsp sea salt

2½ cups unbleached all-purpose flour

2 cups store-bought or homemade pumpkin purée (page 36)

1 (300-mL) can sweetened condensed milk

3 eggs

2 tsp ground ginger

These decadent squares are packed with lots of nutty pecans to balance the sweetness of the caramel. The shortbread base creates a nice, firm foundation with a buttery crumb, making them a favourite with adults and children alike.

CARAMEL-PECAN SQUARES

MAKES 1 (9 × 13-INCH) PAN OF SQUARES

BASE

1½ cups (3 sticks) butter, room temperature, plus extra for greasing

¾ cup sifted icing sugar

½ tsp sea salt

3 cups unbleached all-purpose flour

TOPPING

¾ cup (1½ sticks) butter

1½ cups packed brown sugar

½ tsp salt

½ cup honey

3 Tbsp whipping (36%) cream

2 cups chopped pecans

BASE Preheat the oven to 350°F. Line a 9 × 13-inch baking pan with parchment paper, allowing paper to come up the sides of the pan.

In a large bowl, cream butter, icing sugar and salt. Stir in flour until just combined. Press the mixture into the bottom of the prepared pan. Chill for at least 15 minutes.

Place the pan on the centre rack and bake for 15–20 minutes, until firm and golden brown. Remove from the oven and set aside.

TOPPING Melt butter in a medium saucepan over medium heat. Add sugar, salt, honey and cream and, using a wooden spoon, stir until the mixture comes to a boil. Stop stirring and allow to boil for 30 seconds, then remove from the heat and stir in chopped pecans.

Pour the mixture evenly over the baked base and bake for 20 minutes until the squares are gently bubbling throughout.

Remove from the oven and set aside to cool completely. Transfer to a cutting board by lifting the parchment paper. With a sharp knife, cut into squares.

During the summer, we have a plentiful bounty of raspberries here on the island, so I make my own raspberry jam. These fuss-free squares are just as delicious with a good-quality store-bought jam, though, since the jam is sandwiched between a crisp shortbread base and a rich coconut macaroon topping.

RASPBERRY-COCONUT SQUARES

MAKES I (9 × 13-INCH) PAN OF SQUARES

BASE

1 cup (2 sticks) butter, room temperature, plus extra for greasing

½ cup sifted icing sugar

½ tsp salt

2¼ cups unbleached all-purpose flour

TOPPINGS

1 cup raspberry jam

3½ cups unsweetened shredded coconut

¾ cup egg whites

Finely grated zest and juice of 1 lemon

1¼ cups sugar

¼ cup corn syrup

2 Tbsp butter

2 Tbsp water

Pinch of salt

Preheat the oven to 350°F. Grease a 9 × 13-inch baking pan.

In a large bowl, cream butter, icing sugar and salt. Stir in flour until the mixture is crumbly. Press evenly into the bottom of the prepared pan. Chill for 10 minutes.

Bake on the bottom rack for 15 minutes. Move to the centre rack and bake for 5–8 minutes or until crust turns lightly golden. Remove from the oven and set aside to cool.

Reduce oven temperature to 300°F.

Spread jam evenly over baked crust and chill in the fridge for at least 15 minutes.

In a large bowl, combine coconut, egg whites and lemon juice and zest and mix well. Set aside.

In a saucepan on low heat, combine sugar, corn syrup, butter, water and salt. Stir continuously until the mixture is hot. Pour the hot mixture into the bowl with the coconut and stir until well mixed. Dab coconut topping over jam and spread evenly, keeping the jam layer intact.

Bake on the centre rack for 25 minutes or until coconut macaroon topping is golden. Remove from oven and set aside to cool. Slice, then serve.

An almond shortbread base makes an elegant foundation for tender plums baked in rich, creamy custard. Plums and almonds are perfect partners, but you could easily use other tree fruits, such as sliced apples, pears, apricots or peaches, instead.

ALMOND-PLUM SQUARES

MAKES 1 (9 × 13-INCH) PAN OF SQUARES

BASE Preheat the oven to 350°F. Grease a 9 × 13-inch baking pan.

In a bowl, cream butter, sugar and zest. Add ground almonds, flour and salt and stir until combined. Press the mixture evenly into the bottom of the prepared pan. Chill for 10 minutes.

Place the pan on the bottom rack of the oven and bake for 15 minutes. Move the pan to the centre rack and bake for another 10–15 minutes, or until lightly golden. Remove from oven and set aside to cool.

CRUMB TOPPING In a medium bowl, cream butter, sugar and zest. Stir in flour, sliced and ground almonds, and salt. Set aside.

CUSTARD AND PLUM LAYER In a large bowl, combine flour, sugar, ground almonds, baking powder, orange zest and eggs and mix well.

Lay plums over cooled base, cut-side down. Pour custard evenly over plums and sprinkle the crumb topping overtop. Bake on centre rack of oven for 20–25 minutes, until firm and golden. Remove from the oven and set aside to cool, then cut into squares.

BASE
¾ cup (1½ sticks) butter, room temperature, plus extra for greasing
¾ cup packed brown sugar
1 Tbsp finely grated orange zest
½ cup ground almonds
1½ cups unbleached all-purpose flour
Pinch of salt

CRUMB TOPPING
¼ cup (½ stick) butter, room temperature
½ cup sugar
2 tsp finely grated orange zest
½ cup unbleached all-purpose flour
½ cup sliced almonds
½ cup ground almonds
Pinch of salt

CUSTARD AND PLUM LAYER
½ cup unbleached all-purpose flour
½ cup sugar
½ cup ground almonds
½ tsp baking powder
1 Tbsp finely grated orange zest
4 eggs, beaten
4 cups pitted and halved ripe prune plums

This wonderfully chewy square—with its cake-like base
and sweet, fudgy maple frosting—is sheer decadence
in a baking pan. And it's one treat even celiacs can enjoy—
although if you don't want to use the gluten-free flour blend,
you can still make this with unbleached all-purpose flour
(just increase the amount by three tablespoons).

GLUTEN-FREE COCONUT-WALNUT SQUARES

MAKES I (9 × I3-INCH) PAN OF SQUARES

CAKE Preheat the oven to 350°F. Grease a 9 × 13-inch baking pan.

In a large bowl, whisk together flour blend, walnuts, coconut, baking powder and salt.

Pour melted butter into a large bowl, add sugar and mix well. Whisk in eggs. Stir the mixture into the dry ingredients and mix well until combined. Pour into the prepared pan and level with an offset spatula.

Bake on the bottom rack for 15 minutes. Move the pan to the centre rack and bake for another 15 minutes. Remove from the oven and set aside to cool.

CAKE
¾ cup (1½ sticks) butter, melted, plus extra for greasing

1½ cups Gluten-Free Flour Blend (page 24)

1¼ cups chopped walnuts

½ cup unsweetened shredded coconut

1 Tbsp baking powder

½ tsp sea salt

3 cups packed brown sugar

3 eggs

FROSTING

½ cup (1 stick) butter

¾ cup packed brown sugar

¼ cup whipping (36%) cream

2 Tbsp maple syrup

1½ cups sifted icing sugar

FROSTING In a small saucepan, melt butter over medium heat and stir in brown sugar. Bring to a boil, then remove from heat. Stir in cream and maple syrup.

Put icing sugar into a large bowl, then add half the mixture and stir until smooth. Add the remaining mixture and stir again until smooth.

Pour the frosting over the cake and tilt the pan to evenly distribute. Set aside to cool completely, then slice.

GLUTEN-FREE

Gluten-free batter and dough can be stickier than regular batter. Be sure to scrape down the sides of the bowl as you mix and blend.

This classic North American dessert, also known
as matrimonial cake in Western Canada, dates back to
the 1920s and 1930s—but it's even more popular today.
These date squares have a rich date filling that's brightened
with a hint of citrus, which makes for a nice contrast
to the crisp oatmeal base and topping.

DATE SQUARES (MATRIMONIAL CAKE)

MAKES I (9 × 13-INCH) PAN OF SQUARES

1½ cups (3 sticks) butter, room temperature, plus extra for greasing

5 cups chopped dates

1 orange, peeled, seeded and puréed

1 cup water

2¼ cups unbleached all-purpose flour

1½ cups packed brown sugar

1½ tsp baking powder

1 tsp baking soda

½ tsp salt

2¼ cups rolled oats

Preheat the oven to 350°F. Lightly grease a 9 × 13-inch baking pan.

In a medium saucepan, combine dates, orange purée and water. Cover and cook over low heat for about 10 minutes, or until the dates have softened. Be careful not to let them scorch—turn down heat if it gets too hot. Turn off heat and set dates aside, covered, for 10 minutes.

Using a potato masher, blend the dates until smooth. Set aside to cool.

In a large bowl, whisk flour, sugar, baking powder, baking soda and salt. Add butter and work in with fingers until incorporated, but not pasty. Add oats and, using your hands, incorporate until the mixture is crumbly.

Press half of the oatmeal crumble mixture evenly into the bottom of the prepared pan. Spoon date filling over base and spread evenly. Cover date filling with remaining oatmeal crumble. Pat down gently.

Bake on the bottom rack for 20 minutes. Move the pan to the centre rack and bake for 10 minutes, until golden. Set aside to cool, then cut and serve.

MUFFINS, LOAVES AND BREAKFAST BAKES

MORNINGS ARE GENTLE here on Salt Spring Island. Songbirds gradually wake to the warm sunlight streaming across the Salish Sea, first in a pale glow, then a golden burst of light. There's no rush to greet the day; we just gradually ease into it. It helps that we can start our mornings with these sweet bakes. Here, I've gathered some great muffins and quick breads that are easy to grab on your way out the door, as well as a fantastic granola and—for Sunday mornings, when you have time to spend with the family—the best buttermilk pancakes you can imagine.

This loose and healthy granola is not overly sweet or clumpy—it's more like a muesli. Making your own means you know what goes in it. I usually have it with yogurt and milk, but you could also add fresh fruit.

SIMPLY GRANOLA

MAKES 12–18 SERVINGS

1 cup chopped pecans

1 cup pumpkin seeds

½ cup sesame seeds

12 cups rolled oats

¼ cup (½ stick) butter

¼ cup fresh orange juice

¼ cup honey

½ tsp salt

2 cups unsweetened shredded coconut

1 cup dried cranberries

1 Tbsp ground cinnamon

Preheat the oven to 300°F. Line 2 baking sheets with parchment paper.

Place pecans, pumpkin seeds and sesame seeds onto one of the prepared baking sheets and toast for 10–12 minutes, until fragrant and golden. (Stir at least once to ensure even browning.) Remove pan from oven and set aside to cool.

Put rolled oats into a bowl, add toasted ingredients and stir to combine.

Melt butter in a small saucepan over low heat. Remove from heat and stir in orange juice, honey and salt. Pour the mixture into the dry ingredients bowl and stir until evenly incorporated.

Divide granola between the prepared trays. Return to the oven and bake for 20 minutes, stirring on occasion, until dry.

Pour warm granola back into a large bowl and stir in coconut, cranberries and cinnamon. Set aside to cool and then store in an airtight container for up to 4 weeks.

My dad made these pancakes when I was a little girl,
and to me, they were a treat just for sleepy Sunday mornings.
They are a thicker pancake, but very light, fluffy and tender.
The best rule of thumb with pancakes is that your griddle can't be
too hot or too cold—and don't rush them! Allow the pancake
to cook on one side before turning it. You'll know it's ready to flip
when you see edges form and bubbles break on the surface.

SUNDAY BUTTERMILK PANCAKES

SERVES 4–6

In a large bowl, whisk flour, baking powder, baking soda and salt.

In another bowl, combine buttermilk, eggs and butter and mix well. Pour the wet mixture into the dry ingredients and stir until just combined. Do not overmix.

Heat a large non-stick frying pan over medium heat. Splash with a drop of water—the pan is hot enough if the water sizzles and evaporates quickly.

Add 1 Tbsp of oil to the pan and tilt to coat. When it is hot, ladle in batter in ½-cup measurements, making sure not to crowd the pan.

Cook pancakes until edges begin to set and bubbles pop on surface. Place blueberries or sliced banana onto pancake, then flip and cook until the bottom is golden. Serve immediately with salted butter and maple syrup.

1½ cups unbleached all-purpose flour

2 tsp baking powder

1 tsp baking soda

Pinch of salt

2 cups buttermilk

2 eggs

2 Tbsp butter, melted

Vegetable oil, for frying

1 cup fresh blueberries or 1 sliced banana

Salted butter and maple syrup, to serve

On Salt Spring Island, we have dozens of heritage orchards dating back to the 1860s. More than 450 varieties of apples grow here, ranging from early ripening Wynoochee to late season Calville Blanc d'Hiver—there's even an annual apple festival in early fall. Naturally, those apples find their way into goodies at the bake shop, including these simple, wholesome and delicious muffins.

APPLE-OATMEAL MUFFINS

MAKES 12 MUFFINS

½ cup vegetable oil, plus extra for greasing

2 cups unbleached all-purpose flour

1¼ cups packed brown sugar

1½ tsp ground cinnamon

2 tsp salt

1½ tsp baking powder

1 tsp baking soda

2 apples, cored and coarsely grated

2 cups buttermilk

2 eggs

2½ cups rolled oats

Preheat the oven to 350°F. Grease a 12-cup muffin pan or use paper liners.

In a large bowl, whisk flour, brown sugar, cinnamon, salt, baking powder and baking soda. Stir in grated apples.

In another bowl, combine buttermilk, oil and eggs and mix well. Stir in rolled oats and set aside for 5 minutes to soak.

Pour the wet mixture into the dry-mixture bowl and stir until just combined.

Divide the batter among the prepared muffin cups, filling each three-quarters full. Bake on the bottom rack for 12 minutes. Move the pan to the centre rack and bake for 10–15 minutes, until muffins are firm to the touch or until a skewer inserted in the centre comes out clean. Set aside to cool or serve warm.

TO FREEZE

Cool muffins completely, then put them into zip-top freezer bags and freeze for up to 3 months. To serve, thaw muffins at room temperature or wrap them in foil and heat them in a 350°F oven for 10–15 minutes.

These sophisticated muffins delicately balance the intense flavour of dark chocolate with the hearty texture of oatmeal. They offer all the pleasures of dessert, while providing all the health benefits and slow-release energy of nutrient-rich oats.

COCOA-OATMEAL MUFFINS

MAKES 12 MUFFINS

Preheat the oven to 350°F. Grease a 12-cup muffin pan or use paper liners.

In a large bowl, whisk flour, sugar, cocoa, baking powder, baking soda and salt. Stir in chocolate chips.

In another bowl, beat eggs, buttermilk and oil. Stir in rolled oats and set aside for 5–10 minutes to soak.

Pour the wet mixture into the dry-mixture bowl and stir until just combined.

Divide the batter among the prepared muffin cups, filling each three-quarters full. Bake on the bottom rack for 12 minutes, then move the pan to the centre rack and bake for 10–15 minutes, until muffins are firm to the touch or until a skewer inserted in the centre comes out clean. Set aside to cool or serve warm.

½ cup vegetable oil, plus extra for greasing

2 cups unbleached all-purpose flour

1½ cups packed brown sugar

½ cup Dutch process cocoa powder, sifted (see Note, page 45)

2 tsp baking powder

1 tsp baking soda

½ tsp salt

½ cup chocolate chips

2 eggs

1½ cups buttermilk

1 cup rolled oats

TO FREEZE

Cool muffins completely, then put them into zip-top freezer bags and freeze for up to 3 months. To serve, thaw muffins at room temperature or wrap them in foil and heat them in a 350°F oven for 10–15 minutes.

Even though I was a little girl when my father passed,
I still remember the raisin-bran muffins he used to make.
The molasses and buttermilk make these rich, moist and flavourful.
(And super-nutritious, too.) You can also store the batter
in the fridge for up to two weeks in an airtight container—
just scoop and bake the muffins as you need them!

RAISIN-BRAN MUFFINS

MAKES 24 MUFFINS

2 cups raisins

4 cups bran

4 cups buttermilk

2 Tbsp baking soda

1 cup vegetable oil, plus
    extra for greasing

1 cup fancy molasses

4 eggs

3½ cups unbleached
    all-purpose flour

1 cup packed brown sugar

1 tsp salt

Soak raisins in hot water until plump, about 5 minutes. Drain and set aside.

Preheat the oven to 350°F. Grease a 12-cup muffin pan or use paper liners.

In a large bowl, mix bran, buttermilk, baking soda, oil, molasses and eggs. Set aside.

In another bowl, whisk flour, brown sugar and salt. Pour wet ingredients into dry ones, add raisins and stir until smooth. (You can refrigerate the batter in an airtight container for up to 2 weeks. Stir gently before using.)

Divide the batter among the prepared muffin cups, filling each to the top. Bake on the bottom rack for 12 minutes. Move the pan to centre rack and bake for another 10–15 minutes, until muffins are firm to the touch or until a skewer inserted in the centre comes out clean. Set aside to cool or serve warm.

TO FREEZE

Cool muffins completely, then put them into zip-top freezer bags and freeze for up to 3 months. To serve, thaw muffins at room temperature or wrap them in foil and heat them in a 350°F oven for 10–15 minutes.

I searched for a good cornmeal muffin recipe for a very long time. My first memory of a cornmeal muffin was at a restaurant called Mars in Toronto in the 1970s. It was so good, I've been trying to recreate it ever since. I often find cornmeal muffins to be dry and bland, but these are moist and flavourful and burst with the bright taste of blueberries.

BLUEBERRY-CORNMEAL MUFFINS

MAKES 12 MUFFINS

Preheat the oven to 350°F. Grease a 12-cup muffin pan or use paper liners.

In a large bowl, whisk flour, sugar, baking powder, baking soda and salt. Stir in blueberries.

In another bowl, beat egg, buttermilk, oil, honey and lemon zest. Stir in cornmeal and set aside for 10 minutes to soak.

Pour the wet mixture into the dry-mixture bowl and fold until just combined.

Divide the batter among the prepared muffin cups, filling each three-quarters full. Bake on the bottom rack for 12 minutes. Move the pan to the centre rack and bake for another 10–15 minutes, until muffins are firm to the touch or until a skewer inserted in the centre comes out clean. Set aside to cool or serve warm.

⅓ cup vegetable oil, plus extra for greasing

1½ cups unbleached all-purpose flour

½ cup sugar

1½ tsp baking powder

½ tsp baking soda

½ tsp salt

1 cup fresh or frozen blueberries (not defrosted)

1 egg

2 cups buttermilk

2 Tbsp liquid honey

Finely grated zest of 1 lemon

1½ cups cornmeal

TO FREEZE

Cool muffins completely, then put them into zip-top freezer bags and freeze for up to 3 months. To serve, thaw muffins at room temperature or wrap them in foil and heat them in a 350°F oven for 10-15 minutes.

Cranberry and orange is such a great flavour combination, that alone would make these muffins irresistible. But the oatmeal crumble puts them right over the top. British Columbia is one of the world's largest producers of cranberries, so they're a great local ingredient. Even if you don't love them for their bright, tart flavour, you've got to appreciate how good they are for you—they're considered a superfood and simply loaded with vitamins and antioxidants.

CRANBERRY-ORANGE CRUMBLE MUFFINS

MAKES 12–18 MUFFINS

¾ cup vegetable oil, plus extra for greasing

1 large orange

2 cups fresh or frozen cranberries (not defrosted)

4¼ cups unbleached all-purpose flour

2 cups packed brown sugar

1½ tsp baking soda

½ tsp salt

2 eggs

2 cups buttermilk

1 quantity Oatmeal Crumble (page 28)

TO FREEZE

Cool muffins completely, then put them into zip-top freezer bags and freeze for up to 3 months. To serve, thaw muffins at room temperature or wrap them in foil and heat them in a 350°F oven for 10–15 minutes.

Preheat the oven to 350°F. Grease two 12-cup muffin pans or use paper liners.

Using a paring knife, trim ends from orange (but do not peel it). Cut into quarters, seed and trim membrane. Put orange wedges (with the peel) into a food processor and purée until smooth. Scrape the orange purée into a small bowl and set aside.

Add cranberries to the food processor and pulse 2–3 times, just enough to crack the cranberries. Set aside.

In a large bowl, whisk flour, brown sugar, baking soda and salt. Stir in cranberries.

In another bowl, beat eggs, buttermilk, oil and orange purée. Pour this mixture into the flour mixture and stir until just combined.

Divide the batter among the prepared muffin cups, filling each three-quarters full. Top each muffin with a small handful of oatmeal crumble. Bake on the bottom rack for 12 minutes. Move pans to the centre rack and bake for 10–15 minutes, until muffins are firm to the touch or until a skewer inserted in the centre comes out clean. Set aside to cool or serve warm.

These are one of our top sellers. People like that they're not too sweet and you can really taste the lemon. They have lemon zest in the batter, but they're also dipped in lemon syrup for added citrusy flavour.

LEMON–POPPY SEED MUFFINS

MAKES 12–18 MUFFINS

Preheat the oven to 350°F. Grease two 12-cup muffin pans or use paper liners.

In a large bowl, whisk flour, poppy seeds, baking powder and salt.

In another bowl, whisk eggs, buttermilk, sugar, oil, honey and lemon zest. Fold the mixture into the dry ingredients until just combined.

Divide the batter among the prepared muffin cups, filling each three-quarters full. Bake on the bottom rack for 12 minutes. Move pans to the centre rack and bake for another 10–15 minutes, until muffins are firm to the touch or until a skewer inserted in the centre comes out clean. Set aside to cool.

When muffins are still warm but cool enough to handle, dip tops of muffins into a bowl of lemon syrup. Serve.

1 cup vegetable oil, plus extra for greasing

3 cups unbleached all-purpose flour

¼ cup poppy seeds (see Note)

1 Tbsp baking powder

½ tsp salt

4 eggs

1½ cups buttermilk

1 cup sugar

½ cup honey

Finely grated zest of 1 lemon

Lemon Syrup (page 27), warmed

POPPY SEEDS

Poppy seeds are delicious, but they become rancid quite quickly if not stored properly. Keep them in the freezer rather than a cupboard, and you'll extend their life significantly. In fact, you should keep all nuts and seeds in the freezer if you don't plan to use them right away.

TO FREEZE

Cool muffins completely, then put them into zip-top freezer bags and freeze for up to 3 months. To serve, thaw muffins at room temperature or wrap them in foil and heat them in a 350°F oven for 10–15 minutes.

These savoury zucchini muffins are ideal for a light lunch, perhaps alongside a garden-fresh salad and a glass of rosé. The texture is almost quiche-like, and the garlic and basil add a wonderful Mediterranean flavour. They're also one of the best things you can make when you have a bumper crop of zucchini, which is a regular occurrence here on the island come July and August.

SAVOURY ZUCCHINI MUFFINS

MAKES 12–18 MUFFINS

Preheat the oven to 350°F. Grease a 12-cup muffin pan or use paper liners.

In a small bowl, combine zucchini, onion, garlic, lemon zest and basil and mix well. Cover and set aside.

In a large bowl, whisk flour, sugar, baking powder, baking soda, pepper and salt. Stir in Parmesan until well mixed.

In another small bowl, beat eggs and olive oil.

Make a well in the centre of the dry ingredients and pour in the egg and zucchini mixtures. Starting from the outside in, fold the batter and stir until just combined.

Divide the batter among the prepared muffin cups, filling each three-quarters full. Bake on the bottom rack for 15 minutes. Move the pan to the centre rack and bake for 10–15 minutes, until muffins are firm to the touch or until a skewer inserted in the centre comes out clean. Set aside to cool.

When muffins are cool enough to handle, remove them from the pans as they may sweat as they cool. Serve warm.

½ cup extra-virgin olive oil, plus extra for greasing

2 small zucchinis, coarsely grated and drained in a colander

1 small onion, finely chopped

1 large clove garlic, crushed

Finely grated zest of 1 lemon

1 small bunch fresh basil, finely chopped

2 cups unbleached all-purpose flour

2 Tbsp sugar

2 tsp baking powder

1 tsp baking soda

1 tsp ground black pepper

1 tsp sea salt

1 cup grated Parmesan cheese

6 eggs

TO FREEZE

Cool muffins completely, then put them into zip-top freezer bags and freeze for up to 3 months. To serve, thaw muffins at room temperature or wrap them in foil and heat them in a 350°F oven for 10–15 minutes.

I fell in love with ginger while I lived in the Caribbean, and the spice is at its best in this loaf. It's delicately warming, not too sweet and very tender. It would be delicious with a drizzle of lemon syrup (page 27), salted caramel sauce (page 27) or even vanilla custard (page 35) poured on top.

GINGERBREAD LOAF

MAKES 1 (9 × 5-INCH) LOAF

Butter, for greasing

1½ cups unbleached all-purpose flour

2 tsp baking soda

2 tsp ground ginger

1 tsp ground cinnamon

½ tsp sea salt

2 eggs

1 cup packed brown sugar

⅔ cup vegetable oil

¼ cup fancy molasses

2 tsp freshly grated ginger

¾ cup strong coffee, cooled

Preheat the oven to 350°F. Grease a 9 × 5-inch loaf pan.

In a large bowl, whisk flour, baking soda, spices and salt.

In a separate bowl, beat eggs, brown sugar, oil, molasses and ginger.

Using a spatula, fold in half the egg mixture into the dry ingredients and stir until smooth. Stir in the remaining egg mixture, followed by the coffee. Stir batter gently, until smooth. (Batter will be runny.)

Pour batter into the prepared pan. Bake on the bottom rack for 30 minutes. Move pan to the centre rack and bake for another 30–35 minutes, until firm to the touch or until a skewer inserted in the centre comes out clean. Remove loaf from the pan and set aside for 15 minutes to cool. Slice, then serve.

For a while, we owned a grain mill and made our own flour. In addition to wheat, we milled spelt and discovered that it makes awesome flour for baking. It's not gluten-free, but it's an ancient grain that hasn't been adulterated like wheat has, so it's easier to digest and many people eat it as a wheat alternative. Spelt flour also introduces a nutty flavour that pairs beautifully with the banana in this recipe.

BANANA-SPELT LOAF

MAKES 1 (9 × 5-INCH) LOAF

Preheat the oven to 350°F. Grease a 9 × 5-inch loaf pan.

In a large bowl, whisk flour, baking soda, spices and salt. In a bowl, beat eggs, sugar and oil. Stir in mashed bananas.

Add optional ingredients (if using) to the dry ingredients and mix well. With a spatula, fold the banana mixture into the dry ingredients, until the batter is smooth.

Bake on the bottom rack for 30 minutes. Move the pan to the centre rack and bake for 35–45 minutes, until firm to the touch or until a skewer inserted in the centre comes out clean. Remove loaf from pan, transfer to a cooling rack and set aside to cool, then slice and serve.

Butter, for greasing
2 cups spelt flour
1½ tsp baking soda
1½ tsp ground cinnamon
½ tsp ground nutmeg
½ tsp salt
2 eggs
1¼ cups sugar
⅓ cup vegetable oil
2 cups mashed bananas (about 3 large)

OPTIONAL INGREDIENTS
2 cups unsweetened shredded coconut
2 cups fresh or frozen berries (not defrosted)
2 cups chopped dates
1½ cups chopped pecans or walnuts, toasted

The marriage of spelt, nuts, carrots and spice makes this one of our most popular loaves. It's moist and flavourful, wholesome and simply wonderful. You could put cream cheese frosting (page 26) on this if you wish, but it stands alone perfectly, and deliciously.

CARROT-SPELT LOAF

MAKES 1 (9 × 5-INCH) LOAF

½ cup raisins

Butter, for greasing

½ cup chopped walnuts

2½ cups spelt flour

1 tsp baking powder

1 tsp baking soda

1 Tbsp ground cinnamon

1 tsp ground nutmeg

½ tsp salt

2 cups packed brown sugar

1 cup vegetable oil

4 eggs

2 cups packed finely grated carrots (about 4-6)

Soak raisins in hot water until plump, about 5 minutes. Drain and set aside.

Preheat the oven to 300°F. Grease a 9 × 5-inch loaf pan.

Place chopped walnuts on a baking sheet and bake for 7–10 minutes, until fragrant. Set aside to cool.

Increase oven temperature to 350°F.

In a large bowl, whisk flour, baking powder, baking soda, spices and salt to combine.

In another bowl, beat brown sugar, oil and eggs. Stir in carrots, raisins and walnuts. Add the mixture to the dry ingredients and, using a spatula, fold in until just combined.

Pour batter into the prepared loaf pan. Bake on the bottom rack for 30 minutes. Move the pan to the centre rack and bake for another 40–50 minutes, until firm to the touch or until a skewer inserted in the centre comes out clean. Set aside for 10 minutes to cool in the pan, then remove loaf, slice and serve.

One of the wonders of baking is the way coffee intensifies the flavour of chocolate in baked goods. Here it creates a dark, rich chocolate pound cake that is at once simple and extraordinary. This loaf would be delicious served with your favourite ice cream. Just be sure to use Dutch process cocoa powder for the best flavour and results.

DARK ROAST-CHOCOLATE LOAF

MAKES 1 (9 × 5-INCH) LOAF

Preheat the oven to 350°F. Grease a 9 × 5-inch loaf pan.

In a large bowl, whisk flour, cocoa powder, baking powder, baking soda and salt.

In another large bowl, cream butter and sugar until smooth. Using a whisk, beat in eggs.

Using a spatula, fold half the prepared dry ingredients into the butter mixture until incorporated. Gently stir in coffee until well mixed, then fold in the remaining dry ingredients until batter is smooth.

Pour batter into the prepared pan. Bake on the bottom rack for 30 minutes. Move pan to the centre rack and bake for another 35–40 minutes, or until firm to the touch or until a skewer inserted in the centre comes out clean. Set aside for 10 minutes to cool in the pan, then remove loaf, slice and serve.

¾ cup (1½ sticks) butter, room temperature, plus extra for greasing

2¼ cups unbleached all-purpose flour

1 cup Dutch process cocoa powder, sifted (see Note, page 45)

1½ tsp baking powder

1 tsp baking soda

½ tsp salt

2 cups sugar

2 eggs

2 cups strong coffee, cooled

You rarely see pumpkin and chocolate together in recipes, but you should. The sweet earthiness of pumpkin and the intensity of chocolate make a flavourful combination, and the spelt adds a lovely rich texture. I prefer a semi-sweet chocolate chip that's designed to keep its shape while baking.

PUMPKIN-SPELT LOAF WITH CHOCOLATE CHIPS

MAKES 1 (9 × 5-INCH) LOAF

Preheat the oven to 350°F. Grease a 9 × 5-inch loaf pan.

In a large bowl, whisk flour, baking powder, baking soda, spices and salt.

In another bowl, beat eggs, brown sugar and oil until smooth. Fold in pumpkin purée and chocolate chips until evenly incorporated.

Using a spatula, fold the pumpkin mixture into the dry ingredients until batter is smooth.

Pour the batter into the prepared loaf pan and level with an offset spatula. Bake on the bottom rack for 30 minutes. Move pan to the centre rack and bake for another 40–50 minutes, until firm to the touch or until a skewer inserted in the centre comes out clean. Set aside for 10 minutes to cool in the pan, then remove loaf, slice and serve.

Butter, for greasing

2 cups spelt flour

1½ tsp baking powder

1½ tsp baking soda

2 tsp ground cinnamon

½ tsp ground ginger

½ tsp ground cloves

½ tsp ground nutmeg

½ tsp ground allspice

½ tsp sea salt

3 eggs

1½ cups packed brown sugar

1 cup vegetable oil

1½ cups store-bought or homemade pumpkin purée (page 36)

2 cups chocolate chips

This bread is loaded with wholesome, yummy proteins
in the four different kinds of seeds. The bread is delicate,
but it would be a good sandwich bread with sharp cheddar
and cucumber or even peanut butter. Best of all, because
you're not using yeast as a leavener, it's simple and fast to make.
It should last up to three days—if you don't eat it all first.

MULTISEED
SPELT BREAD

MAKES 1 (9 × 5-INCH) LOAF

Butter, for greasing

½ cup shelled sunflower
  seeds

¼ cup sesame seeds

2½ cups spelt flour

¼ cup ground flaxseed

¼ cup poppy seeds
  (see Note, page 86)

1 tsp baking powder

1 tsp baking soda

1 tsp salt

1 egg

¼ cup liquid honey

1½ cups buttermilk

¼ cup vegetable oil

Preheat the oven to 300°F. Grease a 9 × 5-inch loaf pan.
Spread out sunflower and sesame seeds on a baking
sheet. Toast for 10–12 minutes or until fragrant. Remove from
oven and set aside to cool.

Increase oven temperature to 350°F.

In a large bowl, whisk flour, cooled seeds, flaxseed, poppy
seeds, baking powder, baking soda and salt.

In a small bowl, beat egg, honey, buttermilk and oil. Pour
the mixture into the dry ingredients and, using a spatula, stir
until evenly combined.

Pour batter into the prepared loaf pan and level with an
offset spatula. Bake on the the bottom rack for 30 minutes.
Move pan to the centre rack and bake for another 30–40 minutes, until firm to the touch or until a skewer inserted in the
centre comes out clean. Remove loaf from the pan, then set
aside for 10 minutes to cool. Slice, then serve.

The debate rages on: Is "scone" pronounced with a long o like moan and groan, or a short o like on or mom? My mother told me it was pronounced with a short o, so scawn it is! Scones can be either savoury, as on page 99, or sweet like they are here. With the sweet ones, you can use a myriad of different fruits, including grated apples, cranberries or raspberries, and even add white chocolate to the mix.

BLUEBERRY-LEMON SCONES

MAKES 12–15 SCONES

Preheat the oven to 375°F. Line a baking sheet with parchment paper.

In a small bowl, beat eggs, buttermilk and lemon zest. Chill until ready to use.

In a large bowl, whisk flour, sugar, baking powder and salt. Using a pastry blender, cut butter into flour until it is pea sized. Stir in blueberries.

Make a well in the centre of the flour mixture and pour in the egg mixture. With a spatula, stir from outside edge to centre of the bowl, in quick strokes, until the dough just comes together. Using your hands, gently push together to form a dough.

With a large ice cream scoop, scoop scones onto the prepared baking sheet. Refrigerate for 10 minutes.

Remove baking sheet from the fridge and lightly sprinkle scones with sugar. Bake on the bottom rack for 20 minutes. Move the baking sheet to the centre rack and bake for 15–20 minutes, until scones are firm to the touch. Transfer scones from the baking sheet to a cooling rack. Serve warm with butter.

2 eggs

1½ cups buttermilk

Finely grated zest of 1 lemon

6 cups unbleached all-purpose flour

¾ cup sugar, plus extra for sprinkling

2 Tbsp baking powder

1 tsp salt

1½ cups (3 sticks) cold butter, cut into cubes, plus extra for serving

2 cups fresh or frozen blueberries (not defrosted)

TO FREEZE

Cool scones completely, then put them into zip-top freezer bags and freeze for up to 1 month. To serve, thaw scones at room temperature for 1 hour, then heat them in a 300°F oven for 5–10 minutes.

Tart apples and the tangy bite of sharp cheddar
were just meant for each other. Here the savoury flavours are
complemented with fragrant thyme fresh from the garden.

APPLE, CHEDDAR AND THYME SCONES

MAKES 12–15 SCONES

2 eggs

1½ cups buttermilk

Finely grated zest of
1 lemon

6 cups unbleached
all-purpose flour

¼ cup sugar

2 Tbsp baking powder

1 tsp salt

1½ cups (3 sticks) cold
butter, cut into cubes,
plus extra for serving

1 cup grated sharp cheddar

1 large apple, cored and
coarsely grated

2 Tbsp fresh thyme leaves

TO FREEZE

Cool scones completely, then put them into zip-top freezer bags and freeze for up to 1 month. To serve, thaw scones at room temperature for 1 hour, then heat them in a 300°F oven for 5-10 minutes.

Preheat the oven to 375°F. Line a baking sheet with parchment paper.

In a small bowl, combine eggs, buttermilk and lemon zest and mix well. Chill until ready to use.

In a large bowl, whisk flour, sugar, baking powder and salt. Using a pastry blender, cut butter into flour until it is pea sized. Stir in cheddar, apple and thyme until evenly incorporated.

Make a well in the centre of the flour mixture and pour in the egg mixture. With a spatula, stir from outside edge to centre of the bowl, in quick strokes, until the dough just comes together. Using your hands, gently knead until you have a dough.

With a large ice cream scoop, scoop scones onto the prepared baking sheet. Refrigerate for 10 minutes.

Remove the baking sheet from the fridge. Bake on the bottom rack for 20 minutes. Move the baking sheet to the centre rack and bake for 15–20 minutes, until firm to the touch. Transfer scones from the baking sheet to a cooling rack. Serve warm with butter.

I don't sell doughnuts in my shop, but I used to make them back when I was wheeling my cart around Toronto Island. This dough doesn't require yeast, and it makes an old-fashioned cake doughnut that is super-satisfying. Don't be intimated by frying the batter— it's much easier than you think.

PUMPKIN DOUGHNUTS

MAKE 12–20 DOUGHNUTS

In the bowl of a stand mixer fitted with a paddle attachment, cream sugar and shortening until smooth. Beat in egg yolks. In a separate bowl, whisk flour, baking powder, salt and spices.

In a third bowl, combine sour cream and pumpkin purée and mix well.

In alternating measures, stir the pumpkin mixture and dry ingredients into the egg mixture until you have a sticky, uniform dough. Transfer the dough to a clean bowl, cover with plastic wrap and refrigerate for at least 2 hours or overnight.

Put the dough on a lightly floured counter. Flour your hands and gently press out the dough. Using a rolling pin, roll the dough to a ½-inch thickness. Dip a doughnut cutter into flour each time (to prevent it from sticking) and cut out doughnuts. Carefully transfer doughnuts to a tray lined with paper towels. Lightly flour counter again and re-roll leftover dough. Cut out more doughnuts.

Pour oil into a deep-sided frying pan or large pot and heat until it reaches a temperature between 325°F and 350°F. Carefully lower 4 doughnuts into oil at a time and fry for 3–4 minutes, until browned on the bottom. Turn over and fry for another 3–4 minutes until golden. (I will often break one in half to ensure it is cooked through.) With a slotted spoon, transfer doughnuts back to the tray lined with paper towels. Set aside to cool slightly.

When they are just cool enough to handle, dip top sides of doughnuts into glaze (if using) to cover and set aside to cool. Alternatively, sprinkle with icing sugar. Serve immediately.

½ cup sugar

3 Tbsp vegetable shortening

3 egg yolks

3 cups unbleached all-purpose flour, plus extra for dusting

1 Tbsp baking powder

1 tsp sea salt

1 tsp ground ginger

1 tsp ground nutmeg

½ tsp ground allspice

1 cup sour cream

¾ cup store-bought or homemade pumpkin purée (page 36)

4 cups vegetable oil, for frying

Pumpkin Glaze (page 28) or sifted icing sugar (optional)

PIES
AND
TARTS

IS THERE ANYTHING as wonderfully satisfying as pie? A crisp, flaky pastry filled with sweet, tender fruit or rich, creamy custard—truly, nothing could be better. It's perhaps my favourite thing to bake, because people love it so. But even though people say things are "easy as pie," many bakers don't think pie is easy at all. In the following pages, I'll prove them wrong, with foolproof pastry and easy fillings like sliced apples, tangy berries and spiced plums. I'll demystify cream pies, and show you how to produce irresistible butter tarts and, for the laziest of days, a fail-safe fruit crisp. These recipes are as simple to make as they are simply delicious.

Back when I was in college, my friend Nancy and I would travel around Ontario, tasting butter tarts everywhere we went. (Ontario, which claims to be the birthplace of the butter tart, now has a butter tart trail, tour and festival.) Ever since, butter tarts have been a fixation of mine, and I've been working to perfect these my entire career. You need a suitable balance of filling to pastry—there's a good one-and-a-half inches of filling in these. And as for the question of whether to include raisins or walnuts, it's all down to preference. (For the record, I prefer raisins.)

BUTTER TARTS

MAKES 12–18 TARTS

Whole-wheat flour, for dusting

1–2 disks chilled Pie Pastry dough (page 18)

1 cup corn syrup

⅔ cup packed brown sugar

¼ cup (½ stick) cold butter, cut into cubes

1 tsp vanilla extract or rum

½ tsp sea salt

3 eggs, beaten

¼–½ cup raisins or walnuts (optional)

TO FREEZE

After the butter tarts are baked, set aside to cool. Place tarts in an airtight container and freeze for up to 3 months. When ready to serve, remove tarts from the container and thaw at room temperature. Warm in a 325°F oven for 15 minutes, or until heated through.

Preheat the oven to 350°F.

Dust a counter and top side of pastry with flour and gently roll out pastry dough to form a circle. Press together any cracks that may form at the edges before and while rolling. Shift the pastry circle from time to time to prevent it from sticking to the counter. Turn pastry over, dust with more flour and roll to a ¼-inch thickness. Cut pastry into circles 4–4½ inches in diameter. Gently press and fit into 12-cup tart or muffin pans.

Pour corn syrup into a medium saucepan over medium-low heat, add brown sugar and stir occasionally, until sugar has melted. (Do not allow the syrup to get too hot, or it may turn to candy.)

Remove from heat. Stir in butter, vanilla or rum and salt, until butter has melted. Once syrup has cooled, whisk in beaten eggs, a little at a time, until well incorporated.

Divide raisins or walnuts (if using) evenly between the pastry-lined cups. Pour in syrup mixture, filling each three-quarters full. Bake on the bottom rack for 12 minutes, or until pastry is golden. Move pans to the centre rack and bake for another 10 minutes, until tarts have just begun to puff up and filling has just set. (I like the filling to be neither liquid nor dry. Finding the balance with temperature and baking time gives it a soft finish.) Set aside to cool. Remove tarts from tins, then serve.

With its fruit filling and crunchy topping, a crisp is
sweetly satisfying, easy-breezy to make and the perfect solution
when guests are coming over and you need a quick dessert.
Use seasonal fruit, fresh from the tree or frozen from the previous
season—you don't need to thaw it, as long as the pieces are small
enough. Berries, plums, peaches, rhubarb, pears, apples or a
mixture all make great fillings. You can also freeze crumble for later.

SEASONAL FRUIT CRISP

MAKES 1 (9 × 13-INCH) PAN OF FRUIT CRISP

Preheat the oven to 350°F. Grease a 9 × 13-inch baking
pan or baking dish.

Put all ingredients except for the crumble into a
large bowl and stir well to coat fruit. Pour the mixture into
the prepared pan and place on a baking sheet to protect your
oven in case the juices spill out.

Bake on the bottom rack for 20 minutes. Move the
baking sheet and the pan to the centre rack and bake for
another 15 minutes, until fruit just begins to boil. Bake for
another 5 minutes, if needed. You want to get past the stage
where the liquid will take over the crumble, so the topping
will be supported by the thickening fruit mixture and still
have time to brown. Remove from oven.

Top with oatmeal or cinnamon crumble and press
down gently. Return the pan and the baking sheet to the
centre rack and bake for another 20 minutes, or until
the crumble is golden and juices are boiling. Set aside
to cool slightly, then serve.

Butter, for greasing

6 cups mixed fruit

¾–1 cup sugar, plus extra
if fruit is tart

¼ cup cornstarch

½ tsp freshly grated ginger

Pinch of ground allspice or
nutmeg

Finely grated zest and juice
of 1 lemon

Splash of brandy (optional)

Pinch of sea salt

½ quantity Oatmeal
Crumble (page 28) or
Cinnamon Crumble
(page 29)

TO FREEZE

After the fruit crisp is baked,
set aside to cool. Insert pan
into an extra-large zip-top
freezer bag, seal and freeze
for up to 3 months. When
ready to serve, remove crisp
from the bag and thaw at
room temperature. Warm in
a 325°F oven for 15 minutes,
or until heated through.

With so many different apples on Salt Spring,
I like to use a variety in this classic crumble—there are
always plenty to choose from! It's best to mix a tart apple
with a sweeter one, if you have the option.

APPLE CRISP

MAKES I (9 × I3-INCH) PAN OF FRUIT CRISP

Preheat the oven to 350°F. Grease a 9 × 13-inch baking pan or baking dish.

Put apples into a large bowl, add sugar, cornstarch, spices, salt, lemon zest and juice, and brandy (if using). Stir well to coat. Pour the mixture into the prepared pan and place on a baking sheet to protect your oven in case the juices spill out.

Bake on the bottom rack for 20 minutes. Move the baking sheet and the pan to the centre rack and bake for another 15 minutes, until fruit just begins to boil. Cook for another 5 minutes, if needed. You want to get past the stage where the liquid will take over the crumble, so the topping will be supported by the thickening fruit mixture and still have time to brown. Remove from oven.

Top with oatmeal or cinnamon crumble and press down gently. Return the pan and the baking sheet to the centre rack and bake for another 20 minutes, until the crumble is golden and juices are boiling. Serve warm with vanilla custard.

Butter, for greasing

8-10 medium apples, peeled, cored and sliced (6-7 cups)

¾-1 cup sugar

¼ cup cornstarch

1 tsp ground cinnamon

Pinch of ground nutmeg

Pinch of sea salt

Finely grated zest and juice of 1 lemon

Splash of brandy (optional)

½ quantity Oatmeal Crumble (page 28) or Cinnamon Crumble (page 29)

Vanilla Custard (page 35), warm, to serve

TO FREEZE

After the apple crisp is baked, set aside to cool. Insert pan into an extra-large zip-top freezer bag, seal and freeze for up to 3 months. When ready to serve, remove crisp from the bag and thaw at room temperature. Warm in a 325°F oven for 15 minutes, or until heated through.

My middle names—Marie Claire—are in honour of my grandmothers. It seemed appropriate to name this pie for them, too. Apple pie was one of the very first things I baked with my mom, and that's where it all started, baking with my mom in her kitchen. Back in Ontario, I'd use Northern Spy apples, but here on Salt Spring, I like to use three or four varieties. That way there's a more interesting balance of flavours and textures: sweet and tart, firm and juicy. If you like, serve this pie with a scoop of vanilla ice cream.

APPLE PIE MARIE CLAIRE

MAKES 1 (10-INCH) PIE

Whole-wheat flour, for dusting

2 disks chilled Pie Pastry dough (page 18)

5-6 apples, peeled, cored and sliced (1½-2 lbs) (see Note)

Finely grated zest and juice of 1 lemon

1 cup packed brown sugar

¼ cup cornstarch

1 Tbsp ground cinnamon

Pinch of sea salt

2 Tbsp butter

1 Tbsp rum or whisky (optional)

1 egg, beaten with a splash of cream or milk

Fine or coarse sugar, for sprinkling

APPLES

For this recipe, firmer apples can be sliced thinner than softer apples.

Dust a counter and the top side of a pastry disk with flour and gently roll out pastry to form a circle. Press together any cracks that may have formed at edges before and while rolling. Shift the pastry circle from time to time to prevent it from sticking to the counter. Turn pastry over, dust with more flour and roll into a 12-inch circle. Place pie plate upside down over pastry and trim edges to a ½–1-inch overhang. (Before trimming pastry, ensure it is loosened from the counter.)

Lift finished pastry circle, centre over pie plate and fit it snugly into the bottom and up the sides of plate, checking your overhang is even. Refrigerate for at least 10 minutes.

Dust the counter and the second pastry disk with flour. Press together any cracks that may form at edges before and while rolling. Roll into a 12-inch circle and set aside.

In a large bowl, combine apples, lemon juice and zest, brown sugar, cornstarch, cinnamon, salt, butter and rum or whisky (if using). Using a paring knife, slice apples randomly throughout the bowl a few times. (I find it's a way of further blending flavours and creating random sizes to fill the pie shell.) Stir again.

Pour apples and juices into the chilled pastry shell. Using yours hands, push apples into empty spaces, shaping them into a dome.

continued...

Carefully centre top pastry on pie. Gently press into place from top of dome to edges. Press bottom and top edges together and crimp using fingers. Alternatively, for a lattice top, use a pastry wheel to slice the circle into 10 long strips, ¾–1 inch in width. Begin with one strip down the centre, then a second strip across. Repeat with strips on either side of centre strip, weaving strips to form lattice, 5 vertical and 5 horizontal. Trim strips to meet bottom crust. Press together firmly and roll edge slightly inwards for an even edge, before crimping. Brush top of pie lightly with prepared egg wash and sprinkle with either fine or coarse sugar.

Preheat the oven to 375°F.

Place pie on a baking sheet to catch juices that boil over. Bake on the bottom rack for 40 minutes. (Making sure the bottom crust is properly baked is the reason we start on the bottom rack at a high temperature. If the pie is browning too fast, reduce the oven temperature. Knowing your oven is key to achieving the best results.)

Reduce oven temperature to 350°F and move pie to the centre rack. Bake for another 30–40 minutes or until juices are clear, thick and bubbling. Set pie aside to cool.

Mixing rhubarb with strawberries is the classic combination,
but it turns out that rhubarb is even better with blueberries. Its bright,
tart flavour blends beautifully with the mild sweetness of the blueberries.
Besides, both freeze well, and if you keep some on hand, you can
whip this pie together in an instant. Just remember: when working with
frozen fruit, bake from frozen and only allow for minimal thawing.
(Using frozen fruit keeps it cleaner and easier to prepare.)

BLUE-BARB PIE

MAKES I (10-INCH) PIE

Dust a counter and the top side of a pastry disk with flour and gently roll out pastry to form a circle. Press together any cracks that may have formed at edges before and while rolling. Shift the pastry circle from time to time to prevent it from sticking to the counter. Turn pastry over, dust with more flour and roll into a 12-inch circle. Place pie plate upside down over pastry and trim edges to a ½–1-inch overhang. (Before trimming pastry, ensure it is loosened from the counter.)

Lift finished pastry circle, centre over pie plate and fit snugly into the bottom and up the sides of the plate, checking your overhang is even. Refrigerate for at least 10 minutes.

Dust the counter and the second pastry disk with flour. Press together any cracks that may form at edges before and while rolling. Roll into a 12-inch circle and set aside.

In a large bowl, combine blueberries, rhubarb, sugar, cornstarch, crystallized and fresh ginger, nutmeg and lemon zest and juice.

Pour the mixture and juices into the chilled pastry shell. Using your hands, push the mixture into empty spaces, shaping it into a dome.

Whole-wheat flour, for dusting

2 disks chilled Pie Pastry dough (page 18)

3 cups fresh or frozen blueberries (not defrosted)

2 cups fresh or frozen chopped rhubarb (not defrosted)

1 cups sugar

⅓ cup cornstarch

¼ cup finely chopped crystallized ginger

1 tsp freshly grated ginger

Pinch of ground nutmeg

Finely grated zest and juice of 1 lemon

1 egg, beaten with splash of cream or milk

Fine or coarse sugar, for sprinkling

TO FREEZE

After the pie is baked, set aside to cool. Insert pie into an extra-large zip-top freezer bag, seal and freeze for up to 3 months. When ready to serve, remove pie from the bag and thaw at room temperature. Warm pie in a 325°F oven for 15 minutes, or until heated through.

Carefully centre top pastry on pie. Gently press into place from top of dome to edges. Press bottom and top edges together and crimp using fingers. Alternatively, for a lattice top, use a pastry wheel to slice the circle into 10 long strips, ¾–1 inch in width. Begin with one strip down the centre, then a second strip across. Repeat with strips on either side of centre strip, weaving strips to form lattice, 5 vertical and 5 horizontal. Trim strips to meet bottom crust. Press together firmly and roll edge slightly inwards for an even edge, before crimping. Brush top of pie lightly with prepared egg wash and sprinkle with either fine or coarse sugar.

Preheat the oven to 375°F.

Place pie on a baking sheet to catch juices that boil over. Bake on the bottom rack for 40 minutes. (Making sure the bottom crust is properly baked is the reason we start on the bottom rack at a high temperature. If the pie is browning too fast, reduce the oven temperature. Knowing your oven is key to achieving the best results.)

Reduce oven temperature to 350°F and move pie to the centre rack. Bake for another 30–40 minutes or until juices are clear, thick and bubbling. Set pie aside to cool.

Wonderful red and green grapes grow all over Salt Spring Island. I've tried but could not quite pin down the variety so I just call them "backyard grapes." They freeze beautifully, but have a very delicate flavour so they need a little boost from something else, like the plums here. Since you probably can't get hold of our grapes, you can use any small, seedless eating grapes you like.

PLUM-GRAPE PIE

MAKES 1 (10-INCH) PIE

Dust a counter and the top side of the pastry with flour and gently roll out a pastry disk to form a circle. Press together any cracks that may have formed at edges before and while rolling. Shift the pastry circle from time to time to prevent it from sticking to the counter. Turn pastry over, dust with more flour and roll into a 12-inch circle. Place pie plate upside down over pastry and trim edges to a ½–1-inch overhang. (Before trimming pastry, ensure it is loosened from the counter.)

Lift finished pastry circle, centre over pie plate and fit snugly into the bottom and up the sides of the plate, checking your overhang is even. Refrigerate for at least 10 minutes.

Dust the counter and the second pastry disk with flour. Press together any cracks at edges before and while rolling. Roll into a 12-inch circle and set aside.

In a large bowl, combine plums, grapes, sugar, cornstarch, ginger, nutmeg, brandy (if using) and lemon zest and juice, and mix well.

Pour the mixture and juices into the chilled pastry shell. Using your hands, push fruit into empty spaces, shaping it into a dome.

Whole-wheat flour, for dusting

2 disks chilled Pie Pastry dough (page 18)

3 cups sliced purple plums

2 cups small seedless grapes

1 cup sugar, plus extra for sprinkling

⅓ cup cornstarch

1–2 tsp freshly grated ginger

Pinch of ground nutmeg

Splash of brandy (optional)

Finely grated zest and juice of 1 lemon

1 egg, beaten with splash of cream or milk

Fine or coarse sugar, for sprinkling

Carefully centre top pastry on pie. Gently press into place from top of dome to edges. Press bottom and top edges together and crimp using fingers. Alternatively, for a lattice top, use a pastry wheel to slice the circle into 10 long strips, ¾–1 inch in width. Begin with one strip down the centre, then a second strip across. Repeat with strips on either side of centre strip, weaving strips to form lattice, 5 vertical and 5 horizontal. Trim strips to meet bottom crust. Press together firmly and roll edge slightly inwards for an even edge, before crimping. Brush top of pie lightly with prepared egg wash and sprinkle with either fine or coarse sugar.

Preheat the oven to 375°F.

Place pie on a baking sheet to catch juices that boil over. Bake on the bottom rack for 40 minutes. (Making sure the bottom crust is properly baked is the reason we start on the bottom rack at a high temperature. If pie is browning too fast, reduce oven temperature. Knowing your oven is key to achieving the best results.)

Reduce oven temperature to 350°F and move pie to the centre rack. Bake for another 30–40 minutes, or until juices are clear, thick and bubbling. Set pie aside to cool.

It seems just about everything grows here on the island, including sour cherries and apricots, which also happen to be delicious together. The tartness of the cherries lifts the mild sweetness of the apricots, and all of it is given a gentle kick by the crystallized ginger.

SOUR CHERRY–APRICOT PIE WITH GINGER

MAKES 1 (10-INCH) PIE

Dust a counter and the top side of the pastry with flour and gently roll out a pastry disk to form a circle. Press together any cracks that may have formed at edges before and while rolling. Shift the pastry circle from time to time to prevent it from sticking to the counter. Turn pastry over, dust with more flour and roll into a 12-inch circle. Place pie plate upside down over pastry and trim edges to a ½–1-inch overhang. (Before trimming pastry, ensure it is loosened from the counter.)

Lift finished pastry circle, centre over pie plate and fit snugly into the bottom and up the sides of the plate, checking your overhang is even. Refrigerate for at least 10 minutes.

Dust the counter and the second pastry disk with flour. Press together any cracks at edges before and while rolling. Roll into a 12-inch circle and set aside.

In a large bowl, combine cherries, apricots, crystallized ginger, cornstarch, nutmeg, lemon zest and juice and brandy (if using).

Pour the mixture and juices into the chilled pastry shell. Using your hands, push fruit into empty spaces, shaping into a dome.

Whole-wheat flour, for dusting

2 disks chilled Pie Pastry dough (page 18)

2 cups sour cherries, pitted

2 cups pitted, sliced apricots

¼ cup chopped crystallized ginger

⅓ cup cornstarch

Pinch of ground nutmeg

Finely grated zest and juice of 1 lemon

Splash of brandy (optional)

1 egg, beaten with splash of cream or milk

Fine or coarse sugar, for sprinkling

TO FREEZE

After the pie is baked,
set aside to cool.
Insert pie into an
extra-large zip-top
freezer bag, seal
and freeze for up to
3 months. When ready
to serve, remove
pie from the bag
and thaw at room
temperature. Warm
pie in a 325°F oven
for 15 minutes, or until
heated through.

Carefully centre top pastry on pie. Gently press into place from top of dome to edges. Press bottom and top edges together and crimp using fingers. Alternatively, for a lattice top, use a pastry wheel to slice the circle into 10 long strips, ¾–1 inch in width. Begin with one strip down the centre, then a second strip across. Repeat with strips on either side of centre strip, weaving strips to form lattice, 5 vertical and 5 horizontal. Trim strips to meet bottom crust. Press together firmly and roll edge slightly inwards for an even edge, before crimping. Brush top of pie lightly with prepared egg wash and sprinkle with either fine or coarse sugar.

Preheat the oven to 375°F.

Place pie on a baking sheet to catch juices that boil over. Bake on the bottom rack for 40 minutes. (Making sure the bottom crust is properly baked is the reason we start on the bottom rack at a high temperature. If the pie is browning too fast, reduce oven temperature. Knowing your oven is key to achieving the best results.)

Reduce oven temperature to 350°F and move pie to centre rack. Bake for another 30–40 minutes, or until juices are clear, thick and bubbling. Set pie aside to cool.

THE PURSUIT OF (PIE) PERFECTION

Working with my hands and connecting to the ingredients is one of my greatest pleasures when baking and I feel privileged to do it every day. At the shop, I prefer my bakes to be simple and I keep decorations to a minimum so that the flavours truly speak for themselves. But I also relish those moments of baking at a more leisurely pace—when I get to really explore my creativity and experiment.

When an occasion calls for something a bit more special, a decorative topping can add visual and textural interest to a pie. Sure, it requires a bit of practice, but that extra effort will go a long way in leaving a lasting impression and guests will appreciate your time in going that extra mile.

CUT-OUTS

Cookie cutters make a quick and effective option when decorating pies. I particularly enjoy using a leaf-shaped cookie cutter in autumn to echo the beautiful foliage surrounding us on the island, but you can use just about any shape: circles, hearts, diamonds, etc. Simply fill your pie with the filling, then add a whole lid. Cut out a few decorative shapes to be accents on top. If you want to make a pie topping entirely out of cut-outs, I recommend starting on the outer edge and working your design towards the centre. In both cases, brush the entire pie with an egg wash and sprinkle with coarse sugar, if desired.

BRAID

Cover an entire pie or simply adorn the edge with a decorative braid. Roll your pastry to a thickness of ¼ inch, then cut three long strips, ⅜-inch-wide, and braid them together. Fill your pie with the filling and decorate with the braid. To cover the entire pie, start at the centre, coil the braid and work your way to the outer edge (you will need more braided pastry strips). Trim the braid, brush the entire pie with an egg wash and sprinkle with coarse sugar, if desired.

TWISTS

Similar to the braid, but much easier, this decorative topping involves twisting long strips of pastry across the pie. Roll your dough to a thickness of ¼ inch, then cut into 16–18 long strips, ½ inch wide. Fill your pie with the filling. Begin by giving a pastry strip a few twists, then anchor it on the edge of the pie. Twist it a few more times and press onto the opposite edge. Continue with other strips until the pie is covered, then use the same method to cover with twists crosswise. Brush the entire pie with an egg wash and sprinkle with coarse sugar, if desired.

PIE TOPPINGS

CUT-OUTS

BRAID

TWISTS

One year, for her birthday, my assistant Diana asked for
a pie made with peaches, apricots and yellow plums.
What a wonderful idea, I thought. These are all light,
bright, golden fruits, and the result looks just like sunshine.

SUNSHINE PIE

MAKES 1 (10-INCH) PIE

Dust a counter and the top side of the pastry with flour and gently roll out a pastry disk to form a circle. Press together any cracks that may have formed at edges before and while rolling. Shift the pastry circle from time to time to prevent it from sticking to the counter. Turn pastry over, dust with more flour and roll into a 12-inch circle. Place pie plate upside down over pastry and trim edges to a ½–1-inch overhang. (Before trimming pastry, ensure it is loosened from the counter.)

Lift finished pastry circle, centre over pie plate and fit snugly into the bottom and up the sides of the plate, checking your overhang is even. Refrigerate for at least 10 minutes.

Dust the counter and the second pastry disk with flour. Press together any cracks at edges before and while rolling. Roll into a 12-inch circle and set aside.

In a large bowl, combine peaches, plums, apricots, sugar, cornstarch, crystallized ginger, nutmeg, salt, lemon zest and juice and brandy (if using). Pour the mixture and juices into the chilled pastry shell. Using your hands, push fruit into empty spaces, shaping it into a dome.

Whole-wheat flour, for dusting

2 disks chilled Pie Pastry dough (page 18)

2 cups sliced peaches

1½ cups sliced yellow plums

1 cup sliced apricots

1¼ cups sugar

⅓ cup cornstarch

¼ cup chopped crystallized ginger

Pinch of ground nutmeg

Pinch of sea salt

Finely grated zest and juice of 1 lemon

Splash of brandy (optional)

1 egg, beaten with splash of cream or milk

Fine or coarse sugar, for sprinkling

Carefully centre top pastry on pie. Gently press into place from top of dome to edges. Press bottom and top edges together and crimp using fingers. Alternatively, for a lattice top, use a pastry wheel to slice the circle into 10 long strips, ¾–1 inch in width. Begin with one strip down the centre, then a second strip across. Repeat with strips on either side of centre strip, weaving strips to form lattice, 5 vertical and 5 horizontal. Trim strips to meet bottom crust. Press together firmly and roll edge slightly inwards for an even edge, before crimping. Brush top of pie lightly with prepared egg wash and sprinkle with either fine or coarse sugar.

Preheat the oven to 375°F.

Place pie on a baking sheet to catch juices that boil over. Bake on the bottom rack for 40 minutes. (Making sure the bottom crust is properly baked is the reason we start on the bottom rack at a high temperature. If pie is browning too fast, reduce oven temperature. Knowing your oven is key to achieving the best results.)

Reduce oven temperature to 350°F and move pie to centre rack. Bake for another 30–40 minutes or until juices are clear, thick and bubbling. Set pie aside to cool.

This is not quite a "bumbleberry" pie—it would need apples and rhubarb for that—but a true berry pie that just happens to be our most popular classic. If I can't get the berries from one of the local farmers, then I just ask the neighbours. Someone's sure to have a bunch of berries from their yard put away in the freezer.

TRIPLE BERRY PIE

MAKES 1 (10-INCH) PIE

Dust a counter and the top side of the pastry with flour and gently roll out a pastry disk to form a circle. Press together any cracks that may have formed at edges before and while rolling. Shift the pastry circle from time to time to prevent it from sticking to the counter. Turn pastry over, dust with more flour and roll into a 12-inch circle. Place pie plate upside down over pastry and trim edges to a ½–1-inch overhang. (Before trimming pastry, ensure it is loosened from the counter.)

Lift finished pastry circle, centre over pie plate and fit snugly into the bottom and up the sides of the plate, checking your overhang is even. Refrigerate for at least 10 minutes.

Dust the counter and the second pastry disk with flour as needed. Press together any cracks at edges before and while rolling. Roll into a 12-inch circle and set aside.

In a large bowl, combine berries, sugar, cornstarch, ginger, nutmeg and lemon zest and juice. Pour the mixture and juices into the chilled pastry shell. Using your hands, push berries into empty spaces, shaping them into a dome.

Whole-wheat flour, for dusting

2 disks chilled Pie Pastry dough (page 18)

2 cups raspberries

1½ cups blueberries

1 cup sliced strawberries

1 cup sugar

⅓ cup cornstarch

1 tsp freshly grated ginger

Pinch of ground nutmeg

Finely grated zest and juice of 1 lemon

1 egg, beaten with splash of cream or milk

Fine or coarse sugar, for sprinkling

TO FREEZE

After the pie is baked, set aside to cool. Insert pie into an extra-large zip-top freezer bag, seal and freeze for up to 3 months. When ready to serve, remove pie from the bag and thaw at room temperature. Warm pie in a 325°F oven for 15 minutes, or until heated through.

Carefully centre top pastry on pie. Gently press into place from top of dome to edges. Press bottom and top edges together and crimp using fingers. Alternatively, for a lattice top, use a pastry wheel to slice the circle into 10 long strips, ¾–1 inch in width. Begin with one strip down the centre, then a second strip across. Repeat with strips on either side of centre strip, weaving strips to form lattice, 5 vertical and 5 horizontal. Trim strips to meet bottom crust. Press together firmly and roll edge slightly inwards for an even edge, before crimping. Brush top of pie lightly with prepared egg wash and sprinkle with either fine or coarse sugar.

Preheat the oven to 375°F.

Place pie on a baking sheet to catch juices that boil over. Bake on the bottom rack for 40 minutes. (Making sure the bottom crust is properly baked is the reason we start on the bottom rack at a high temperature. If pie is browning too fast, reduce oven temperature. Knowing your oven is key to achieving the best results.)

Reduce oven temperature to 350°F and move pie to centre rack. Bake for another 30–40 minutes or until juices are clear, thick and bubbling. Set pie aside to cool.

Pecan pie has a sweet filling similar to butter tarts, but with
a layer of crunchy, toasty nuts that makes it utterly delicious. I've been
making this recipe since I worked at the Senator Restaurant in Toronto
years ago, and it's still one of my favourites. It's wonderfully nutty,
and only better with a spoonful (or two) of whipped cream.

PECAN PIE

MAKES 1 (10-INCH) PIE

Dust counter and the top side of the pastry with flour and gently roll out a pastry disk to form a circle. Press together any cracks that may have formed at edges before and while rolling. Shift the pastry circle from time to time to prevent it from sticking to the counter.

Turn pastry over, dust with more flour and roll into a 12-inch circle. Place pie plate upside down over pastry and trim edges to a 1-inch overhang. (Before trimming pastry, ensure it is loosened from the counter.)

Lift finished pastry circle, centre over pie plate and fit snugly into the bottom and up the sides of the plate, checking your overhang is even. Fold overhang under, creating a doubled-up edge. Press together and crimp, making a decorative fluted edge. Refrigerate for at least 10 minutes.

Preheat the oven to 350°F.

In a bowl, whisk brown sugar and flour.

Pour melted butter to a 2-cup measuring cup and add corn syrup. Add to bowl of brown sugar and whisk to combine. Add eggs, lemon zest, vanilla and salt and mix well.

Sprinkle pecans into chilled pie shell and pour filling over pecans. They will float to the top.

Place pie on a baking sheet and bake on the bottom rack for 25 minutes. Move pie to the centre rack and bake for 25–30 minutes, until filling is puffed and set. Set aside to cool, then slice.

Whole-wheat flour,
  for dusting
1 disk chilled Pie Pastry
  dough (page 18)
1 cup packed brown sugar
2 Tbsp unbleached
  all-purpose flour
¼ cup (½ stick) butter,
  melted
1½ cups corn syrup
6 eggs
1 Tbsp finely grated
  lemon zest
1 tsp vanilla extract
¼ tsp sea salt
2 cups pecans

This is fantastic and rich, filled with gorgeous flavour.
It's quite different from the pecan pie (page 126);
both are delicious, but this one is made even more
decadent with the addition of chocolate and bourbon.

CHOCOLATE-BOURBON-PECAN PIE

MAKES 1 (10-INCH) PIE

Dust a counter and the top side of the pastry with flour and gently roll out the pastry disk to form a circle. Press together any cracks that may have formed at edges before and while rolling. Shift the pastry circle from time to time to prevent it from sticking to the counter.

Turn pastry over, dust with more flour and roll into a 12-inch circle. Place pie plate upside down over pastry and trim edges to a 1-inch overhang. (Before trimming pastry, ensure it is loosened from the counter.)

Lift finished pastry circle, centre over pie plate and fit snugly into the bottom and up the sides of the plate, checking your overhang is even. Fold overhang under, creating a doubled-up edge. Press together and crimp, making a decorative fluted edge. Refrigerate for at least 10 minutes.

Preheat the oven to 350°F.

In a bowl, whisk corn syrup, sugar, bourbon, salt and eggs. Set aside.

Melt butter in a medium saucepan on low heat, add chocolate and stir with a heatproof spatula until chocolate is almost melted. Remove from heat and stir until smooth.

Pour the chocolate into the sugar-egg mixture and stir to combine. Pour into chilled pie crust and evenly sprinkle pecans over the filling.

Bake on the bottom rack for 30 minutes. Move pie to the centre rack and bake for another 20–30 minutes, until filling is just set.

Remove pie from oven and set aside to cool before slicing.

Whole-wheat flour, for dusting

1 disk chilled Pie Pastry dough (page 18)

1 cup corn syrup

1 cup packed brown sugar

¼ cup bourbon

¼ tsp sea salt

4 eggs

¼ cup (½ stick) butter

4 oz unsweetened baking chocolate, chopped (about ¾ cup)

1½ cups pecans, toasted

This comforting old-school classic is like chocolate milk, only better. It's delicious as is, but it's best finished with whipped cream—the lightness of the cream makes a wonderful contrast to the rich depth of the chocolate custard.

CHOCOLATE CREAM PIE

MAKES I (IO-INCH) PIE

Whole-wheat flour, for dusting

1 disk chilled Pie Pastry dough (page 18)

3 cups milk

½ cup + 2 Tbsp sugar, divided

3 egg yolks

⅓ cup cornstarch

¼ cup + 3 Tbsp Dutch process cocoa powder, sifted and divided (see Note, page 45)

½ tsp sea salt

2 oz semi-sweet baking chocolate, chopped (about ½ cup), more shaved chocolate to serve

2 Tbsp butter

1 tsp vanilla extract

1½ cups whipping (36%) cream

Dust a counter and the top side of the pastry with flour and gently roll out the pastry disk to form a circle. Press together any cracks that may have formed at edges before and while rolling. Shift the pastry circle from time to time to prevent it from sticking to the counter.

Turn the pastry over, dust with a little more flour and roll into a 12-inch circle. Place pie plate upside down over pastry and trim pastry to a 1-inch overhang. (Before trimming pastry, ensure it is loosened from the counter.)

Lift finished pastry circle, centre over pie plate and fit snugly into the bottom and up the sides of the plate, checking your overhang is even. Fold overhang under, creating a doubled-up edge. Press together and crimp, making a decorative fluted edge. Set in the freezer for at least 10 minutes.

Preheat the oven to 350°F.

Remove pie shell from freezer. Cut a piece of foil large enough to cover pie shell. Press foil into shell, shaping to fit. Fill with enough dried beans or rice to cover sides of pie shell.

Bake on the bottom rack for 20 minutes. Remove shell from oven and gently lift foil to see if the edges have started to brown, which will mean the pie shell is set enough to remove foil. If it does not look like it is set, return to the oven and bake for another 10 minutes on the bottom rack. Remove pie shell from oven and carefully remove foil and beans.

continued . . .

BLIND BAKING

When you want to fill a pastry crust with a chilled, unbaked filling like chocolate cream, lemon curd (page 135) or maple cream (page 136), you need to bake the crust beforehand. But an unfilled crust can easily burn and become both brittle and bitter. That is why you need to blind bake it. In blind baking, the chilled crust is covered with foil or parchment, which is then filled with light weights such as rice or beans to keep it in place. The covered pie shell goes into the oven and bakes for a time without being exposed to direct heat, so it can set without burning.

Place pie shell on the centre rack and bake for 5–8 minutes, watching carefully, until lightly golden.

In a small saucepan, heat milk until it begins to steam. Remove from heat and set aside.

In a bowl, whisk ½ cup sugar and egg yolks and beat until pale. Add cornstarch, ¼ cup cocoa powder and salt and stir until smooth.

Place a damp towel under the bowl to anchor. Slowly pour hot milk into the egg mixture while whisking. Using a spatula, scrape the mixture into the saucepan and set over medium heat. Stir until custard thickens, then boil for 10 seconds and remove from heat.

Add chocolate, butter and vanilla and stir until melted. Pour into baked pie shell and cover with plastic wrap to prevent skin from forming. Chill.

Beat whipping cream on medium speed until it begins to thicken. Add remaining 2 Tbsp sugar and 3 Tbsp cocoa powder and beat until soft peaks form. Remove plastic wrap from pie and spread whipped cream over pie in peaks and valleys. Cool again before serving.

This is a beautifully spiced version of the autumnal classic. Its rich filling and fragrant seasonings are a reminder of why "pumpkin spice everything" became so popular in the first place. This is the pie you'll want on your table at Thanksgiving—and for just about any occasion.

PUMPKIN PIE

MAKES 1 (10-INCH) PIE

Dust a counter and the top side of the pastry with flour and gently roll out a pastry disk to form a circle. Press together any cracks that may have formed at edges before and while rolling. Shift the pastry circle from time to time to prevent it from sticking to the counter.

Turn pastry over, dust with more flour and roll into a 12-inch circle. Place pie plate upside down over pastry and trim edges to a 1-inch overhang. (Before trimming pastry, ensure it is loosened from the counter.)

Lift finished pastry circle, centre over pie plate and fit snugly into the bottom and up the sides of the plate, checking your overhang is even. Fold overhang under, creating a doubled-up edge. Press together and crimp, making a decorative fluted edge. Refrigerate for at least 10 minutes.

Preheat the oven to 350°F.

In a large bowl, whisk remaining ingredients (except sweetened whipped cream) together until smooth. Pour pumpkin filling into pie shell and bake on the bottom rack for 30 minutes. Move pie to the centre rack and bake for another 15–20 minutes, until filling is just set. (Filling will continue to bake after being removed from the oven, so take this into consideration.) Overbaking will cause the filling to crack. Set aside to cool, then slice and serve with whipped cream.

Whole-wheat flour, for dusting

1 disk chilled Pie Pastry dough (page 18)

1½ cups store-bought or homemade pumpkin purée (page 36)

1 cup evaporated milk

1 cup whipping (36%) cream

3 eggs, beaten

½ cup packed brown sugar

½ cup fancy molasses

2 Tbsp maple syrup

2 Tbsp sugar

1 tsp ground ginger

1 tsp ground cinnamon

½ tsp ground allspice

¼ tsp ground nutmeg

½ tsp vanilla extract

Pinch of sea salt

Sweetened whipped cream, to serve

Lemon lovers will adore this tart. It started out as a lemon
cream pie, but that wasn't quite enough lemon for me. So I put
a layer of lemon curd over the lemon custard, and it was incredible.
I love the way the natural citrus comes through. I recommend
using a fluted tart pan with a removable bottom.

DOUBLE LEMON TART

MAKES 1 (10-INCH) TART

1 quantity Short Crust Pastry dough (page 22)

Whole-wheat flour, for dusting

¾ cup sugar

¾ cup whipping (36%) cream

6 eggs

Finely grated zest and juice of 2 lemons

½ quantity Lemon Curd (page 34)

Sifted icing sugar, to serve

Preheat the oven to 350°F.

Put short crust pastry into a 10-inch fluted tart pan. With floured fingers, press crust evenly into the bottom and up the sides of the pan. Freeze shell for at least 15 minutes.

Remove pie shell from freezer. Cut a piece of foil large enough to cover pie shell. Press foil into shell, shaping to fit. Fill with enough dried beans or rice to cover sides of pie shell.

Bake on the bottom rack for 20 minutes. Remove shell from oven and gently lift foil to see if the edges have started to brown, which will mean the pie shell is set enough to remove foil. If it does not look like it is set, return to the oven and bake for another 10 minutes on the bottom rack. Remove pie shell from oven and carefully remove foil and beans.

Place pie shell on the centre rack and bake for 5–8 minutes, watching carefully, until lightly golden.

Reduce oven temperature to 325°F.

In a bowl, combine sugar, whipping cream, eggs and lemon zest and juice. Pour filling into baked shell and bake on the centre rack for 20–25 minutes, until just set. Set aside for 20 minutes to cool.

While tart is still a little warm, spoon lemon curd over custard and smooth with offset spatula. Place in fridge until completely cooled.

Remove sides of pan easily by placing the pie on top of a large tin. Carefully slide palette knife under crust to loosen from base. Transfer to a large flat plate. Dust with icing sugar before serving.

Years ago, this was one of the pies I chose to teach at a
class at the Urban Element in Ottawa, where my son, Kyle,
was working. I had long forgotten about the pie, but the
class was attended by a relative of a Salt Spring Islander.
I reconnected and had her send me a copy of the recipe.
And yes, she'd kept it all that time—it's that good.

MAPLE CREAM PIE

MAKES I (IO-INCH) PIE

Dust a counter and the top side of the pastry with flour and
gently roll out a pastry disk. Press together any cracks
that may have formed at edges before and while rolling. Shift
the pastry circle from time to time to prevent it from sticking
to the counter. Turn pastry over, dust with more flour and roll
into a 12-inch circle. Place pie plate upside down over pastry
and trim edges to a 1-inch overhang. (Before trimming pastry,
ensure it is loosened from the counter.)

Lift finished pastry circle, centre over pie plate and fit
snugly into the bottom and up the sides of the plate. Fold overhang under, creating a doubled-up edge. Press together and
crimp, making a decorative fluted edge. Set in the freezer for at
least 10 minutes.

Preheat the oven to 350°F.

Remove pie shell from freezer. Cut a piece of foil large
enough to cover pie shell. Press foil into shell, shaping to fit.
Fill with enough dried beans or rice to cover sides of pie shell.

Bake on the bottom rack for 20 minutes. Remove shell
from oven and gently lift foil to see if the edges have started to
brown, which will mean the pie shell is set enough to remove

Whole-wheat flour, for
dusting

1 disk chilled Pie Pastry
dough (page 18)

3 cups light (10%) cream

½ cup maple syrup

½ cup packed brown sugar,
divided

4 egg yolks

⅓ cup cornstarch

½ tsp sea salt

2 Tbsp butter

1 tsp vanilla extract

1 cup whipping (36%) cream

foil. If it does not look like it is set, return to the oven and bake another 10 minutes on the bottom rack. Remove shell from oven and carefully remove foil and beans. Place pie shell on the centre rack and continue baking for 5–8 minutes, watching carefully, until lightly golden.

In a small saucepan, heat light cream until it begins to steam. Remove from heat and set aside.

In a bowl, whisk maple syrup, ¼ cup brown sugar and egg yolks and beat until pale. Whisk in cornstarch and salt until smooth.

Place a damp towel under the bowl to anchor. Slowly pour hot cream into the bowl while whisking. With a spatula, scrape contents back into saucepan and cook over medium heat. Stir until thickened. Allow the mixture to bubble for 10 seconds and remove from heat. Stir in butter and vanilla. Pour into baked pie shell, cover with plastic wrap to prevent skin from forming and chill for at least 2 hours or overnight.

In a cold bowl, beat whipping cream until it begins to thicken. Add remaining ¼ cup brown sugar and beat until firm peaks form. Spoon on top of chilled pie and serve.

"Galette" is a term used in French cuisine for a variety of flat, round cakes and pastries; here it's a rustic, free-form tart that doesn't need a pan—they can be baked right on a baking sheet. Filled with rich, creamy vanilla custard and topped with fruit, it's a lovely combination that's sure to impress.

RUSTIC GALETTES WITH VANILLA CUSTARD AND FRUIT COMPOTE

MAKES 6–8 TARTS

Divide the pastry into 6–8 equal pieces. Form into disks, wrap and chill for 10 minutes. Remove pastry from the fridge and set aside for 15 minutes at room temperature (which makes the pastry easier to roll). Dust a counter and the top of the pastry disks with a little flour. Gently roll disks into 6–7-inch rounds.

Take edge of each round and fold 1½ inches of pastry towards centre, crimping the folds so they will stay together. Freeze tart shells, uncovered, for at least 1 hour, until hard. (If not using right away, transfer shells to an airtight container or zip-top bag and freeze for up to 3 months.)

Preheat the oven to 350°F. Line a baking sheet with parchment paper.

Remove tart shells from freezer and place on the prepared baking sheet, evenly spacing them 2 inches apart. Spoon 3 Tbsp custard into each tart shell. Allow to sit at room temperature for 5 minutes, then gently squeeze edges of each tart shell inwards, so the lip curls in a bit. Bake on the bottom rack for 12–15 minutes, until the tart shell is set and beginning to brown.

Move the tart shells to the centre rack and bake for another 10 minutes, until tarts are golden and puffed.

Remove baking sheet from oven and carefully spoon fruit compote into tarts, covering custard. Bake on the centre rack for 5 minutes. Remove from oven and set aside to cool. Tarts can be served slightly warm with any remaining custard.

1 quantity Buttery Pastry dough (page 20)

Whole-wheat flour, for dusting

1 quantity Vanilla Custard, chilled (page 35)

1 quantity Fruit Compote, chilled (page 36)

CAKES

THERE'S A REASON WHY special occasions call for cake. Cakes are the most magnificent, celebratory bakes anyone can make. They can be elaborate, adorned with swirls of buttercream (page 30) and sandwiched with layers of lemon curd (page 34) or chocolate ganache (page 37). But a cake can be simple and comforting, too, especially if it's a sturdy pound cake (page 145) or one that's loaded with rum-soaked fruit (pages 156 and 159). Whether it's a fancy party or your afternoon coffee break, it's always the right time for cake.

Could there be a tastier way to eat your veggies? Carrot cake
is one of the great classics. The orange root vegetable has been
used as a sweetener in baking since at least medieval times,
when sugar was scarce and expensive whereas carrots were sweet
and plentiful. The earliest recipes for carrot cake date back
to the late nineteenth century, but it became super-trendy in the 1960s—
and its popularity hasn't diminished since. This version is dense
and moist, lightly spiced and perfectly irresistible.

CARROT CAKE

MAKES 1 (9-INCH) 2-LAYER CAKE

Soak raisins in hot water until plump, about 5 minutes.
Drain and set aside.

Preheat the oven to 350°F. Grease two 9-inch round
baking pans.

In a large bowl, whisk sugar and oil together. Beat in eggs.

In another bowl, whisk flour, cinnamon, baking powder,
baking soda, nutmeg and salt.

Pour dry ingredients into wet ingredients, then add carrots,
raisins and walnuts and fold until batter is smooth.

Divide batter between the 2 prepared pans and bake on the
bottom rack for 15 minutes. Move the pan to the centre rack
and bake for another 15–20 minutes, or until firm to the touch.
Remove from oven and set aside to cool.

Finish with cream cheese frosting.

¾ cup raisins

1 cup vegetable oil,
plus extra for greasing

2½ cups packed brown
sugar

4 eggs

2 cups unbleached
all-purpose flour

1 Tbsp ground cinnamon

1 tsp baking powder

1 tsp baking soda

1 tsp ground nutmeg

1 tsp salt

1 lb carrots, grated (about
4 cups)

1 cup chopped walnuts

1 quantity Cream Cheese
Frosting (page 26)

Buttermilk is one of those magic ingredients every baker should stock. It has a bit of acidity that reacts with baking soda to give your bakes a beautiful lift. But it also makes cakes, muffins and loaves rich and moist. This recipe has been in my repertoire for a very long time. The way the layers settle, they're great for icing—they don't dome, so you don't have to slice the tops off.

BUTTERMILK-SPICE CAKE

MAKES 1 (9-INCH) 2-LAYER CAKE OR 1 (9 × 13-INCH) SHEET CAKE

¾ cup (1½ sticks) butter, plus extra for greasing

2¾ cups unbleached all-purpose flour

1½ tsp baking soda

1½ tsp ground cinnamon

¾ tsp ground nutmeg

¼ tsp ground cloves

1 tsp sea salt

1½ cups buttermilk, room temperature

1 Tbsp finely grated lemon zest

2 cups packed brown sugar

3 eggs

1 quantity Chocolate Buttercream (page 31) or Cream Cheese Frosting (page 26)

Preheat the oven to 325°F. Grease two 9-inch round baking pans or a single 9 × 13-inch pan.

In a large bowl, whisk flour, baking soda, spices and salt.

In a small bowl, mix together buttermilk and lemon zest. Set aside.

In the bowl of a stand mixer fitted with a paddle attachment, cream butter and sugar until light and fluffy. Add one egg at a time to the butter mixture, beating well after each addition.

Gently fold in half the flour mixture, mixing until smooth. Pour in the buttermilk mixture, then fold in the remaining flour. Stir until smooth.

Divide batter evenly into the prepared baking pan(s). Level with an offset spatula.

Bake on the bottom rack for 15 minutes. Move pans to the centre rack and bake for another 20–25 minutes, until firm to the touch or until a skewer inserted in the centre comes out clean. Set aside to cool, then remove from the pan(s). Frost with chocolate buttercream or cream cheese frosting and serve.

Traditionally, pound cake was a pound of sugar, a pound of flour, a pound of butter. This version is slightly more refined, and endlessly versatile. You can frost it, drizzle it with lemon syrup (page 27), slather it with fruit preserves or use it as a base for trifle. Or simply enjoy it plain and delicious.

PERFECT POUND CAKE

MAKES 1 (9 × 5-INCH) LOAF

1 cup (2 sticks) butter, room temperature, plus extra for greasing

1¾ cups sugar

1 Tbsp vanilla extract

4 eggs

2¾ cups unbleached all-purpose flour

2 tsp baking powder

1 tsp salt

1 cup sour cream, room temperature

Preheat the oven to 300°F. Grease a 9 × 5-inch loaf pan.

In a bowl, beat butter, sugar and vanilla until light and fluffy. Add one egg at a time to the butter mixture, beating well after each addition.

In a separate bowl, combine flour, baking powder and salt. Fold half the flour mixture into the butter mixture, then stir in sour cream. Fold in remaining flour until batter is smooth.

Pour the batter into the prepared pan and bake on the bottom rack for 40 minutes. Move the pan to the centre rack and bake for another 40 minutes, until firm to the touch or until a skewer inserted in the centre comes out clean.

Remove cake from oven and allow to cool for 10 minutes before removing it from the pan. Slice, then serve.

Could anything be more decadent than a deep, dark,
rich chocolate cake? Not too sweet, layered with
luscious frosting, and surprisingly easy to make, this is
a cake worth celebrating—and worthy of a celebration, too.

CHOCOLATE LAYER CAKE

MAKES 1 (9-INCH) 2-LAYER CAKE

Preheat the oven to 350°F. Grease two 9-inch round baking pans. Cut parchment circles and fit into bottoms of pans.

In a medium bowl, stir coffee and cocoa powder together until well mixed. Set aside.

In the bowl of a stand mixer fitted with a paddle attachment, beat butter, sugar and vanilla until light and fluffy. Scrape bowl to ensure the ingredients are evenly incorporated. Beat eggs in one at a time, scraping bowl after each addition.

In a large bowl, mix flour, baking soda, baking powder and salt.

With a spatula, fold half the flour mixture into the butter mixture. Fold in coffee-cocoa mixture until smooth. Add the remaining flour mixture.

Divide batter evenly into the prepared pans and level with an offset spatula.

Bake on the bottom rack for 15 minutes. Move pans to the centre rack and bake for another 15–20 minutes, until firm to the touch or until a skewer inserted in the centre comes out clean. Set aside to cool, then remove from pans. Frost with your preferred buttercream or chocolate ganache and serve.

1 cup (2 sticks) butter, plus extra for greasing

2 cups coffee, room temperature

1 cup Dutch process cocoa powder, sifted (see Note, page 45)

2½ cups sugar

2 tsp vanilla extract

4 eggs

2¾ cups unbleached all-purpose flour

2 tsp baking soda

½ tsp baking powder

1 tsp salt

1 quantity preferred Buttercream (pages 30–31) or Chocolate Ganache (page 37)

I've loved baking with bananas since I lived in
the Caribbean—their sweet, mild flavour harmonizes
so well with warming spices, as well as nuts and chocolate.
The lovely banana flavour here marries beautifully
with buttercream (page 30) and shredded coconut.

BANANA CAKE

MAKES 1 (9-INCH) 3-LAYER CAKE

Preheat the oven to 350°F. Grease three 9-inch round baking pans. Cut parchment circles and fit into bottoms of pans.

In a large bowl, whisk flour, baking soda, nutmeg and salt and set aside.

In the bowl of a stand mixer fitted with a paddle attachment, cream butter and sugar until light and fluffy. Stir in vanilla, then add eggs, one at a time, beating well after each addition.

In a small bowl, combine mashed bananas and buttermilk and mix well.

With a spatula, gently fold half the flour mixture into the butter mixture and mix until smooth. Fold in the banana-buttermilk mixture. Stir in the remaining flour.

Divide equally into the prepared pans and level with an offset spatula. Bake on the bottom rack for 15 minutes. Move pans to the centre rack and bake for another 20–25 minutes, until firm to the touch or until a skewer inserted in the centre comes out clean. Set aside to cool, then remove from pans.

Frost with buttercream and press shredded coconut onto sides and overtop.

1 cup (2 sticks) butter, room temperature, plus extra for greasing

3½ cups unbleached all-purpose flour

2 tsp baking soda

1 tsp ground nutmeg

½ tsp salt

2 cups sugar

1 tsp vanilla extract

4 eggs

2 cups mashed bananas (about 3 large)

2 cups buttermilk

1 quantity Buttercream (page 30)

Unsweetened shredded coconut, for garnish

If you want to up your dessert game at Thanksgiving, this sweetly spiced cake makes a great alternative to pumpkin pie. But it's also a good choice year-round—the perfect addition to a picnic basket or afternoon tea. You'll need a ten-inch tube pan.

PUMPKIN CAKE WITH SALTED CARAMEL SAUCE

MAKES 1 (10-INCH) TUBE CAKE

Butter, for greasing

2¾ cups unbleached all-purpose flour

2 tsp baking powder

2 tsp baking soda

1 Tbsp ground cinnamon

1 tsp ground ginger

1 tsp ground cloves

1 tsp ground nutmeg

1 tsp ground allspice

1 tsp salt

2 cups packed brown sugar

¾ cup vegetable oil

4 eggs

2 cups store-bought or homemade pumpkin purée (page 36)

2 cups chopped pecans

1 quantity Salted Caramel Sauce (page 27), for drizzling

Preheat the oven to 350°F. Grease a 10-inch tube pan with a removable bottom.

In a large bowl, whisk flour, baking powder, baking soda, spices and salt until well combined.

In a medium bowl, beat together brown sugar, oil and eggs. Stir in pumpkin purée.

Pour wet ingredients into flour mixture, then add pecans and stir until batter is smooth.

Pour the batter into the prepared baking pan. Bake on the bottom rack for 30 minutes. Move pan to the centre rack and bake for another 40–50 minutes, until firm to the touch or until a skewer inserted in the centre comes out clean. If needed, bake for another 10–15 minutes.

Set aside to cool, then remove cake from the pan. Drizzle salted caramel sauce overtop.

This cake makes the most of Salt Spring's famous apples, and I'll use whatever apples are in season. They're all great as far as I'm concerned, except for Red Delicious, which have a softer consistency when baked. You'll need a ten-inch tube pan.

CHUNKY APPLE CAKE

MAKES 1 (10-INCH) TUBE CAKE

Preheat the oven to 350°F. Grease a 10-inch tube pan with a removable bottom.

Put apples into a bowl, add lemon juice and stir. Set aside.

In a large bowl, whisk flour, spices, baking soda and salt.

In a medium bowl, beat brown sugar, butter and oil. Beat in eggs one at a time, scraping down the bowl after each addition. Add vanilla.

With a spatula, fold wet mixture into the dry mixture. Stir in chopped apples.

Pour the batter into the prepared pan and level with an offset spatula.

Bake on the bottom rack for 30 minutes. Move pan to the centre rack and bake for another 40–50 minutes, until firm to the touch or until a skewer inserted in the centre comes out clean. Set aside to cool, then remove cake from the pan. Drizzle salted caramel sauce overtop.

1 cup (2 sticks) butter, room temperature, plus extra for greasing

4-5 cups chopped unpeeled cored apples

2 Tbsp fresh lemon juice

3 cups unbleached all-purpose flour

2 tsp ground cinnamon

½ tsp ground allspice

1 tsp baking soda

1 tsp salt

1½ cups packed brown sugar

¼ cup vegetable oil

3 eggs

1 tsp vanilla extract

1 quantity Salted Caramel Sauce (page 27), for drizzling

A buckle is a super-old-school bake. In my mind, it was named for the way it buckles when you bake it. It's fast, easy and versatile— and a great way to use seasonal fruits. Here on Salt Spring, the first fruit that comes into season is rhubarb, followed by berries and then stone fruits like peaches and plums and, finally, apples and pears. Doesn't matter which is in season; they're all good in this cake.

FRESH FRUIT BUCKLE

MAKES 1 (9 × 13-INCH) SHEET CAKE

1½ cups (3 sticks) butter, room temperature, plus extra for greasing

2¼ cups unbleached all-purpose flour

1½ cups sugar

1 Tbsp baking powder

½ tsp salt

6 eggs

1 tsp vanilla extract

2 lbs fresh fruit, such as apples, pears, peaches or strawberries, unpeeled and chopped into ½-inch cubes

½ quantity Oatmeal Crumble (page 28)

1 quantity Vanilla Custard (page 35), to serve

Preheat the oven to 350°F. Grease a 9 × 13-inch baking pan.
In a large bowl, whisk flour, sugar, baking powder and salt. With a spatula, incorporate butter into the mixture until combined.

In a separate bowl, beat together eggs and vanilla, then pour into the flour-butter mixture. Stir until batter is smooth.

Fold half the fruit into the batter and spread into the prepared pan. Sprinkle remaining fruit evenly over batter, then cover with an even layer of oatmeal crumble.

Bake on the bottom rack for 30 minutes. Move the pan to the centre rack and bake for another 30–40 minutes, until firm to the touch or until a skewer inserted in the centre comes out clean. Set aside to cool before slicing. Serve with vanilla custard on the side.

OUR BEST WHITE CAKE

MAKES 1 (9-INCH) 4-LAYER CAKE

This is my most popular request for wedding cakes. White cake is often dismissed as boring, but not this one. It's almost like a chiffon cake, but not quite as fluffy. It's got good structure, but it's still light. I often put lemon curd in the middle, or fresh berries. You can frost it with buttercream (page 30), chocolate ganache (page 37) or whatever you like. It is especially beautiful when decorated with local flowers.

Preheat the oven to 325°F. Grease four 9-inch round baking pans. Cut parchment circles and fit into bottom of pans.

In a large bowl, whisk flour, baking powder and salt.

In a separate bowl, combine buttermilk and orange zest and juice.

In a third bowl, beat butter, oil, 2 cups sugar and vanilla until light and fluffy.

Gently fold half the flour mixture into the butter mixture. Stir in the buttermilk mixture, followed by the remaining flour mixture. Set aside.

In the bowl of a stand mixer fitted with a whisk attachment, beat egg whites on medium-low speed until soft peaks form. Slowly add remaining 1 cup sugar. Increase speed and beat until peaks are shiny and firm.

Gently fold half the beaten egg whites into the batter to lighten. (Fold gently so as not to knock the air out of the egg whites.) Fold in the remaining egg whites.

Divide batter evenly into the prepared baking pans and level with an offset spatula. Bake on the bottom rack for 20 minutes. Move pans to the centre rack and bake for another 20 minutes, or until firm to the touch. (Cakes will also shrink from sides of the pans when done.) Set aside to cool, then remove from pans. Spread filling between the layers, frost and serve.

¾ cup (1½ sticks) butter, room temperature, plus extra for greasing

5 cups unbleached all-purpose flour

5 tsp baking powder

1½ tsp salt

1½ cups buttermilk

Finely grated zest and juice of 1 orange

¾ cup vegetable oil

3 cups sugar, divided

1 Tbsp vanilla extract

1¼ cups egg whites (about 8), room temperature

LAYER CAKE VARIATIONS

1 LEMON

FILLING: Lemon Curd (page 34)

OUTSIDE: Buttercream (page 30)

TOPPING: Finely grated lemon zest

2 CHOCOLATE DECADENCE

FILLING: Ganache (page 37)

OUTSIDE: Chocolate Buttercream (page 31)

TOPPING: Chocolate shavings

EASTER LAYER CAKE

3 FILLING: Chocolate Buttercream (page 31)

OUTSIDE: Buttercream (page 30)

TOPPING: Toasted unsweetened shredded coconut, mini Cadbury eggs

4 STRAWBERRIES AND CREAM

FILLING: Layer of Buttercream (page 30), then layer of strawberry jam

OUTSIDE: Buttercream (page 30)

TOPPING: Sliced strawberries, sifted icing sugar

5 LAVENDER HONEY CAKE

FILLING: Buttercream (page 30) + 1 Tbsp organic dried lavender

OUTSIDE: Buttercream (page 30)

TOPPING: Organic dried lavender, a drizzle of honey

6 ALMOND AND ORANGE BLOSSOM

FILLING: Buttercream (page 30) + 2 tsp orange blossom water

OUTSIDE: Buttercream (page 30) + 1 Tbsp almond extract

TOPPING: Sifted icing sugar, sliced almonds, edible flowers

OUR BEST WHITE CAKE

LAVENDER
HONEY CAKE

Unlike the dark fruit cake on page 159, this one is
light and more like a super-fruity dense pound cake.
The fruit is still soaked in rum, though, so it has
a wonderfully bright, boozy kick.

FRUIT CAKE, LIGHT AND WONDERFUL

MAKES 3 (9 × 5-INCH) LOAVES

Place all the dried fruit and the crystallized ginger in a large glass jar or ceramic container and stir in ½ cup of the rum and the citrus juices. (Reserve the zests for later.) Cover and store at room temperature overnight, or up to 3 days, stirring every other day. (Alternatively, if the seal on the container is secure, turn every so often.)

Preheat the oven to 300°F. Grease three 9 × 5-inch loaf pans. In a medium bowl, whisk flour, baking powder and salt.

In a large bowl, beat butter, sugar, vanilla and zests until light and fluffy. Beat in eggs and yolks, 2 at a time. Scrape bowl after each addition to ensure the ingredients are evenly incorporated.

Stir in soaked fruit and any liquid, then fold in the flour mixture, pecans and coconut until batter is smooth. Divide batter evenly between the prepared pans and level with an offset spatula. Bake on the centre rack for 50–60 minutes, until firm to the touch or until a skewer inserted in the centre comes out clean.

2 cups dried cranberries

2 cups chopped dried apricots

2 cups golden raisins

2 cups candied citrus peels

2 cups chopped crystallized ginger

1 cup aged rum, divided

Finely grated zest and juice of 1 orange

Finely grated zest and juice of 1 lemon

2 cups (4 sticks) butter, room temperature, plus extra for greasing

3½ cups unbleached
  all-purpose flour

1½ Tbsp baking powder

1¼ tsp salt

2½ cups sugar

1 Tbsp vanilla extract

6 eggs

6 egg yolks

2 cups pecans, lightly
  toasted in the oven,
  cooled and chopped

2 cups unsweetened
  shredded coconut

Remove from oven and drizzle remaining ½ cup rum over hot loaves. Set aside to cool completely. Using plastic wrap, tightly wrap each of the cakes twice, then store them in a cool room for at least 3 days before serving. They store very well because of the rum and, properly wrapped, can last for months.

STORAGE

A fruit cake must age to allow the ingredients to marry and reach its full potential. Store it in a cool, dry place like a pantry or cupboard and trust me—the longer you leave it, the better it will taste!

In the Caribbean, they call this "black cake." It's deep, dark, boozy and sinfully good. Every grandma would make her own black cake and keep it in a tin, bringing it out for special guests. It's worth noting that you will need to soak the dried fruit in the rum well in advance—I soak it upwards of three months but one week will do nicely. Then add more rum to the cake when it's done.

FRUIT CAKE, DARK AND DELICIOUS

MAKES 4 (6-INCH) CAKES

4 cups raisins

4 cups chopped pitted prunes

4 cups chopped dried apricots

2 cups candied citrus peels

2 cups dried cranberries

3 cups aged rum, divided

2 cups (4 sticks) butter, room temperature, plus extra for greasing

3½ cups unbleached all-purpose flour

1 Tbsp ground cinnamon

2 tsp ground allspice

1 tsp ground nutmeg

1 tsp ground cloves

1 Tbsp baking powder

1 tsp baking soda

1 tsp sea salt

½ cup sugar

½ cup packed brown sugar

1½ cups fancy molasses

7 eggs

Place all the dried fruit in a large glass jar or ceramic container and stir in 2 cups of the rum. Cover and store in a cool, dark place for up to 6 months, but at least 1 week. Be sure to stir once a week. (Alternatively, if the seal on the container is secure, turn every so often.)

Preheat the oven to 325°F. Grease four 6-inch round baking pans.

In a large bowl, whisk flour, spices, baking powder, baking soda and salt.

In a separate bowl, beat butter, sugars and molasses until light and fluffy. Beat in eggs, 1–2 at a time. Scrape bowl often to ensure the ingredients are evenly incorporated.

Create a well in the centre of the flour mixture. Pour the butter mixture into centre, followed by the fruit mixture. Using a spatula, fold ingredients together, starting from outside in, until batter is evenly mixed.

Divide batter evenly between prepared baking pans and level with an offset spatula. Bake on the bottom rack for 40 minutes.

Reduce oven temperature to 300°F and move the pan to the centre rack. Bake for another 40–50 minutes, until firm to the touch or until a skewer inserted in the centre comes out clean.

Remove from oven and drizzle remaining 1 cup of rum over-top of the cakes. Set aside to cool completely. Using plastic wrap, tightly wrap the each of the cakes twice, then store them in a cool room for at least 3 days before serving. They store very well because of the rum and, properly wrapped, can last for months.

Here, I've used bright, tart cranberries, making this cake a
wonderful choice for your Thanksgiving and holiday parties.
You can also make it with just about any fruit you like—pineapple,
apples, peaches, plums, whole strawberries, you name it. The best part
is the way the juices from the fruit combine with the sugar and butter
while the cake bakes to create an irresistible caramel topping.

CRANBERRY UPSIDE-DOWN CAKE

MAKES 1 (10-INCH) CAKE

FRUIT BASE Preheat the oven to 350°F. Grease a 10-inch round
baking pan.

Pour melted butter evenly into the prepared pan. Sprinkle
sugar over butter.

In a separate bowl, combine cranberries, ginger and orange
juice, then spread out evenly in the pan. Set aside.

CAKE In a medium bowl, whisk flour, baking powder, baking
soda and salt.

In another bowl, beat butter, sugar and orange zest until
light and fluffy. Beat in eggs, one at a time, and scrape bowl
after each addition to ensure the ingredients are evenly
incorporated.

Pour half the flour mixture into the butter mixture and fold
until combined. Fold in sour cream, followed by the remaining
flour mixture. Stir until combined and batter is smooth.

Drop large spoonfuls of batter into the pan. With an offset
spatula, gently spread batter until fruit is covered.

Bake on the bottom rack for 30 minutes. Move the pan to
the centre rack and bake for another 20–30 minutes, until
firm to the touch or until a skewer inserted in the centre
comes out clean. Set aside to cool for 20 minutes, then invert
onto a cake plate.

FRUIT BASE

¼ cup (½ stick) butter,
melted, plus extra for
greasing

½ cup sugar

4 cups fresh or frozen cranberries (not defrosted)

2 tsp freshly grated ginger

Juice of 1 orange

CAKE

2½ cups unbleached
all-purpose flour

1 Tbsp baking powder

½ tsp baking soda

½ tsp salt

1 cup (2 sticks) butter, room
temperature

1½ cups sugar

1 Tbsp finely grated orange
zest

2 eggs

1 cup sour cream

This is both cake and custard, and perfectly delightful. My mother made this cake, and so did her mother, my Granna. To me, lemon pudding cake is a comforting dessert that simply tastes like home. The key with this recipe is the ratio between the cake and the pudding—you don't want too much (or too little) of either. You'll need a nine-inch Pyrex or ceramic dish, as well as a larger pan for the bain-marie.

MOTHER'S LEMON PUDDING CAKE

MAKES 1 (9-INCH-SQUARE) CAKE

2 Tbsp butter, melted, plus extra for greasing

¾ cup sugar

4 eggs, separated, at room temperature

⅓ cup unbleached all-purpose flour

1 cup milk

⅓ cup fresh lemon juice

Finely grated zest of 2 lemons

Preheat the oven to 350°F. Grease a 9-inch square Pyrex or ceramic baking dish.

Fill a large baking or roasting pan halfway with hot water and place in the oven. (The pan needs to be big enough to hold the smaller baking dish, and the water just deep enough to come halfway up its sides. This is called a bain-marie, and it is the ideal way to bake custards like flans, crème caramels and this cake.)

In the bowl of a stand mixer fitted with a paddle attachment, cream butter and sugar until smooth. Add egg yolks, flour, milk, lemon juice and zest.

In a separate bowl, beat egg whites until stiff peaks form. Gently fold into batter until incorporated. (Fold gently so as not to knock the air out of the egg whites.)

Pour batter into the prepared baking dish and place in hot water bath in the oven. Bake for 40 minutes. Test if the custard is cooked by gently shaking the pan—the cake should jiggle but be firm, not liquid. Remove from the oven and serve.

This cake is so light and fluffy, it's like biting into a lemon-flavoured cloud. It has a delicate structure and gets its lift from two leaveners: a chemical one, baking powder, and a mechanical one, which is egg white. It's more forgiving than an angel food cake, and so good— you'll probably feel as if you could sit down and eat the whole thing. You'll need a ten-inch tube pan with a removable bottom for this recipe.

LEMON CHIFFON CAKE

MAKES 1 (10-INCH) TUBE CAKE

Preheat the oven to 325°F.

In a bowl, whisk flour, ½ cup sugar, baking powder and salt.

In a separate bowl, mix water and lemon juice. Beat in egg yolks, oil and lemon zest. With a spatula, fold the egg mixture into the flour mixture until evenly mixed. Set aside.

In the bowl of a stand mixer fitted with a whip attachment, slowly beat egg whites until frothy. Increase speed and pour in remaining ¼ cup sugar. Beat until firm, moist peaks form.

With a spatula, gently fold in half the egg whites to lighten batter. (Fold gently so as not to knock the air out of the egg whites.) Gently fold in the remaining egg whites until incorporated.

Pour batter into an ungreased straight-sided tube pan (with a removable bottom) and level with an offset spatula. Bake on the centre rack for 1 hour (do not open oven door). Remove cake from oven and set the centre of the tube onto the top of a full tin can, leaving the cake upside down in the pan. (The structure of the cake is so delicate that it must be upside down so it won't collapse into itself.) Allow cake to cool completely before removing from pan.

To loosen the cake, carefully run a palette knife around the perimeter of the pan. Remove outer pan, then run a palette knife along the base of the tube pan to release the cake. Carefully invert cake onto a serving plate, frost with lemon buttercream and serve.

1½ cups unbleached all-purpose flour

¾ cup sugar, divided

1 Tbsp baking powder

½ tsp salt

½ cup water

¼ cup fresh lemon juice

6 eggs, separated

½ cup vegetable oil

1 Tbsp finely grated lemon zest

1 quantity Lemon Buttercream (page 31)

You could, if you wished, make this cheesecake with a cookie-crumb crust, but I love the cakey texture of a streusel pastry. Some cheesecakes come with the fruit on top; here, we've tucked a sour cherry compote (page 36) between the crust and the filling. You'll find tons of sour cherries on Salt Spring Island—if you're lucky enough to beat the birds to them.

CHEESECAKE WITH SOUR CHERRY COMPOTE

MAKES I (10-INCH) CHEESECAKE

1 quantity Streusel Pastry dough (page 22)

3 cups cream cheese, room temperature

1¼ cups sugar

2 Tbsp finely grated lemon zest

1 tsp freshly grated ginger

3 eggs

2 egg yolks

1 cup sour cream

1 quantity Fruit Compote (page 36), made with sour cherries, cooled

Put the dough into a 10-inch springform pan or a round baking pan with a removable bottom. Press the dough evenly three-quarters of the way up the sides of the pan, and evenly into bottom of the pan. Refrigerate until chilled.

Preheat the oven to 350°F.

In the bowl of a stand mixer fitted with a paddle attachment, blend cream cheese until smooth. Beat in sugar, lemon zest and ginger. Beat in eggs and egg yolks, one at a time, until well combined. Stir in sour cream.

Remove crust from fridge, pour in cherry compote and spread evenly. Pour cheesecake filling over the cherries. Bake on the bottom rack for 30 minutes.

Turn oven temperature down to 275°F. Move the pan to the centre rack and bake for 1½ hours, or until cheesecake is set. The centre should be firm to the touch. Turn off oven and, with door slightly ajar, leave cake to cool for 2 hours.

Remove cake from oven, cool completely and refrigerate until ready to serve. Remove the pan from around the cake. Using a palette knife, carefully loosen bottom and slide onto a serving plate.

SAVOURIES

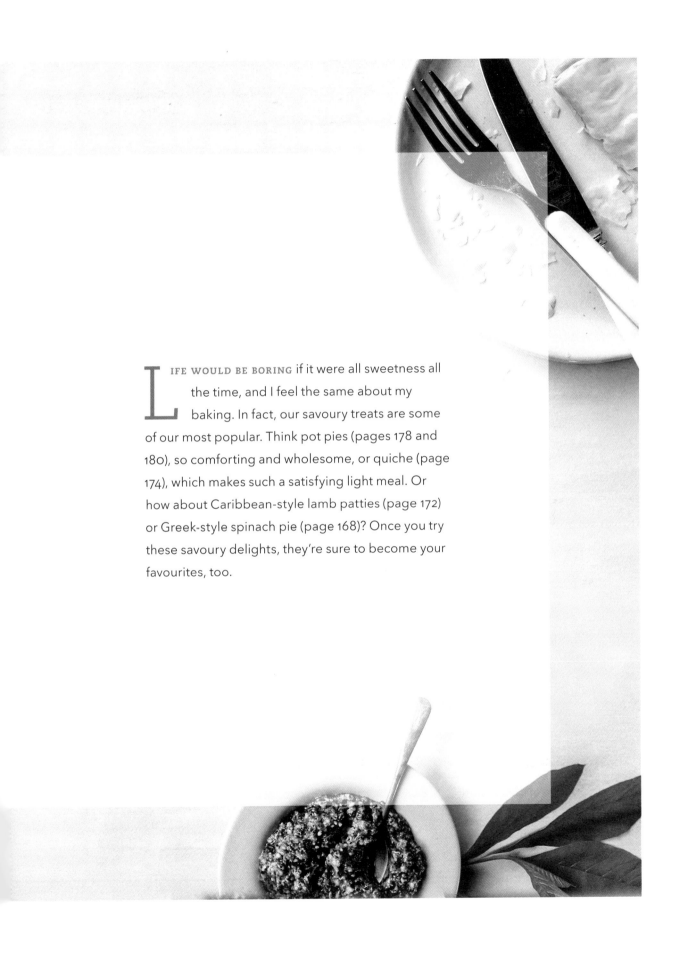

LIFE WOULD BE BORING if it were all sweetness all the time, and I feel the same about my baking. In fact, our savoury treats are some of our most popular. Think pot pies (pages 178 and 180), so comforting and wholesome, or quiche (page 174), which makes such a satisfying light meal. Or how about Caribbean-style lamb patties (page 172) or Greek-style spinach pie (page 168)? Once you try these savoury delights, they're sure to become your favourites, too.

This is a classic phyllo pastry pie stuffed with spinach and feta. I did try making it with nettles one year—they are so prolific on the island—but it takes a ton of work to clean enough of them to go in a pie, and the flavour is so intense, I'm not sure I'd do it again. I use ricotta as well as feta—it has a milder flavour that lets the spinach and flavourings shine, and it gives these hand pies a great texture. Adding to that is the phyllo, which is light, airy and crisp. There are good-quality frozen phyllo pastries available; just handle them with care so they don't tear.

SPANAKOPITA (SPINACH PIE)

MAKES 12 SPANAKOPITA

Melt 1¼ cups (2½ sticks) butter in a small saucepan, then remove from heat and set aside to cool. Chill in the fridge until butter is cold and hard. Make a hole at the edge and drain off the liquid settled on the bottom. The remaining hard butter is the clarified butter. Return saucepan to the stove.

Heat a large frying pan over high heat. When hot, add spinach and drizzle with olive oil. Cover and turn heat off, allowing spinach to steam. (Spinach can be prepped this way the day before and left to sit in a colander to drain overnight.) Squeeze out excess liquid from spinach, transfer to cutting board and roughly chop.

In the same frying pan, melt remaining ½ cup (1 stick) butter over medium heat. Add onions and sauté for 10 minutes, until golden. Stir in flour, salt, pepper, dried herbs, nutmeg and lemon zest and cook for 1 minute. Set aside to cool.

In a large bowl, combine spinach and the onion mixture and mix well. Stir in the cheeses.

Preheat the oven to 350°F. Line a baking sheet with parchment paper.

1¾ cups (3½ sticks) butter, divided

4 lbs fresh spinach, weighed with stems attached; remove stems

Extra-virgin olive oil, for drizzling

1 small onion, finely chopped

¼ cup unbleached all-purpose flour

1 tsp salt

1 tsp ground black pepper

1 tsp dried basil

½ tsp dried oregano

¼ tsp ground nutmeg

Finely grated zest of 1 lemon

2 cups ricotta cheese

1½ cups crumbled feta cheese

2 (454-g) packages phyllo pastry, thawed out in the fridge overnight

Reheat the clarified butter, until melted.

Unwrap phyllo and lay a sheet on the counter. Cover the remaining sheets with a damp towel to keep them from drying out as you work. Brush the sheet with clarified butter and lay a second sheet overtop. Brush only half the sheet from top to bottom and fold sheets over to make 1 long strip.

Place ½ cup filling at the top, flatten filling a little, and fold sides in just enough to enclose edge of filling. Roll the slightly flattened pie, tucking as you go, if necessary, allowing the end to tuck under. Brush with butter. Repeat until all the phyllo or filling has been used.

Place finished pies on the prepared baking sheet and bake on the bottom rack for 15 minutes. Move the baking sheet to the centre rack and bake for 15–20 minutes, until pastry is deep golden. Remove from the oven and serve warm, or set aside to cool.

SPANAKOPITA (PAGE 168)

LAMB PATTIES (PAGE 172)

The pastry I use is based on a Jamaican patty pastry and is uniquely golden due to turmeric. The filling, though, is all Salt Spring. The island is famous for its lamb, which has an exceptionally delicious flavour that's renowned as far as Buckingham Palace—rumour has it that it's the Queen's favourite! There are about a dozen local lamb breeds, the oldest of which, the Suffolk, came to the island around 1890. The quality is also due to the feed: the sweet local hay and grain, as well as foraged wild berries and salal. Some say it's also the result of ocean breezes that leave a fine trace of salt that ends up in the feed and makes the meat so sweet. In any case, it makes a fine lamb patty.

LAMB PATTIES

MAKES 24 PATTIES (OR 36 APPETIZER-SIZED)

In a large bowl, combine lamb, onions, garlic, cilantro, salt, pepper and spices and mix well. Cover and chill in fridge for 2 hours or overnight.

Heat oil in a large frying pan over medium heat. Add lamb mixture and sauté for 20–30 minutes, until browned and cooked through. Remove from heat and stir in rolled oats (they will soak up any excess juices). Fold in grated carrots.

Roll out a portion of the patty dough to a ¼-inch thickness. Use a round object with a sharp edge, such as a top from a canister or a plastic lid, to cut out circles 6 inches in diameter. (For appetizers, cut them to 4 inches.) Repeat with remaining pastry as needed.

Preheat the oven to 375°F. Line a baking sheet with parchment paper.

3 lbs ground lamb

1 medium onion, finely chopped

2 cloves garlic, crushed

½ cup chopped cilantro

2 tsp sea salt

2 tsp ground black pepper

1 tsp ground cumin

1 tsp ground ginger

½ tsp ground allspice

¼ cup vegetable oil

2 cups rolled oats

2 cups grated carrots

1 quantity Patty Pastry dough (page 23)

1 egg

3 Tbsp light (10%) cream

TO FREEZE

Patties can be stored in an airtight container or zip-top freezer bag and frozen for up to 3 months. Bake from frozen on the bottom rack of a 350°F oven for 20 minutes. Move to the centre rack and bake for another 20 minutes, until golden.

With a pastry circle cupped in your hand, add ½–⅔ cup filling. Pinch edges of pastry together to enclose filling in a half-moon-shaped patty. Repeat with remaining pastry circles and filling.

In a small bowl, whisk egg and cream to create an egg wash. Place patties onto the prepared baking sheet and brush lightly with egg wash.

Bake on the bottom rack for 15 minutes or until edges of pastry begin to brown. Move to the centre rack and continue baking until patties are golden. (There's no need to turn them over.) Remove from oven and serve warm, or set aside to cool.

CLASSIC QUICHE

MAKES 1 (10-INCH) QUICHE

Quiche is easy and delicious, and makes for a great light lunch or a breakfast-to-go in your hand. This quiche here is one shareable pie, but at the bake shop we make our quiches in Texas-sized muffin pans, a perfect portion for one.

QUICHE CUSTARD In medium bowl, whisk all ingredients until smooth. Do not overbeat. Set aside.

CLASSIC QUICHE Dust a counter and the top side of pastry with flour and gently roll the pastry disk into a circle. Press together any cracks that may form at edges before and while rolling. Shift the pastry circle from time to time to prevent it from sticking to the counter.

Turn pastry over, dust with more flour and roll into a 12-inch circle. Place pie plate upside down over pastry and trim edges to a 1-inch overhang. (Before trimming pastry, ensure it is loosened from the counter.)

Lift finished pastry circle, centre over pie plate and fit snugly into the bottom and up the sides of the plate. Fold overhang under, creating doubled-up edge. Press together and crimp, making a decorative fluted edge. Set in the freezer for at least 10 minutes.

Preheat the oven to 375°F.

Remove pie shell from freezer. Layer cheddar cheese on bottom of pie shell, followed by the filling of your choice. Pour in quiche custard.

Place quiche on a baking sheet and bake on the bottom rack for 30 minutes. Move to the centre rack and bake for 20 minutes, or until custard is set and puffed.

Set aside to cool for 15 minutes, then slice and serve warm.

QUICHE CUSTARD
1 cup light (10%) cream
5 eggs
Pinch of sea salt
Pinch of ground nutmeg
Pinch of white pepper

CLASSIC QUICHE
Whole-wheat flour, for dusting
1 disk chilled Pie Pastry dough (page 18)
2 cups grated sharp cheddar cheese
Filling of your choice (recipe here)
2 cups Quiche Custard (recipe here)

CUSTARD TIP
People often tell me that the custard makes for the best quiche they've ever had—all you need is cream, eggs and a touch of spice. Just remember to beat the custard until just smooth (do not over-beat); simplicity really is the key here.

MY FAVOURITE QUICHE FILLINGS

1
¼ cup olive oil

2 large onions, thinly sliced

1 cup grated Gruyère

CARAMELIZED ONION AND GRUYÈRE

Heat oil in a large frying pan over medium heat. Add onions and sauté for 10 minutes, until caramelized and golden. Set aside to cool.

Add onions to quiche and top with Gruyère, then follow remaining instructions on facing page.

2
¼ onion, finely chopped

½ red bell pepper, finely chopped

¼ bunch Italian parsley, finely chopped

1 lb quality bacon, cut crosswise into fine slices

BACON COMPOTE

In a large bowl, combine onion, pepper and parsley. Set aside.

Heat a frying pan over medium heat, add bacon and fry for 20 minutes, until cooked but not crispy. Transfer bacon to a colander with a bowl underneath and drain fat.

Add hot bacon to the vegetables and stir until well combined. Add to quiche, then follow remaining instructions on facing page.

3
¼ cup vegetable oil

3 cups chopped mushroom caps, cut into ½-inch dice

½ cup crumbled blue cheese

MUSHROOM–BLUE CHEESE

Heat oil in a large frying pan over medium-high heat. Add mushrooms, reduce heat to low and sauté for 10 minutes, until browned and liquid has evaporated. Set aside to cool.

Add mushrooms to quiche and top with crumbled blue cheese, then follow remaining instructions on facing page.

4
1 cup canned diced tomatoes, drained

1 cup soft goat cheese

¼ cup purchased or homemade pesto

GOAT CHEESE, TOMATO AND PESTO

Add diced tomatoes to quiche and crumble goat cheese overtop. Drizzle with pesto, then follow remaining instructions on facing page.

MUSHROOM–
BLUE CHEESE

CLASSIC QUICHE

GOAT CHEESE,
TOMATO AND PESTO

CARAMELIZED
ONION
AND GRUYÈRE

This is a comfort food favourite—I cannot keep these in stock!
People buy them six at a time, so we're always making more.
In part, it's because the ingredients are just so good. I get my eggs,
chicken, lamb and goat from the same farmer on Salt Spring Island,
and it shows what a difference quality makes. You'll need
six-inch aluminum foil pie pans if you plan to freeze these.

CHICKEN POT PIE

MAKES 10–12 (6-INCH) POT PIES

In a tall and narrow stockpot, combine chicken, celery, carrots, onion and parsley stems. Finely chop parsley leaves and set aside. Pour water into pot and bring to a simmer. Cook for 1 hour, until chicken is cooked through.

Turn off heat. Using tongs, remove chicken and place in a roasting pan to cool. Remove skin and set aside. Remove meat from bones and shred or chop. Refrigerate until needed.

Return bones and skin to warm stock, stir and allow to sit for 30 minutes to 1 hour. Strain into a large bowl.

Ladle 4 cups of stock into a saucepan. (Any leftover stock can be frozen or used for soup.) Bring to a boil over medium heat. Add potatoes and cook for 10 minutes. Add carrots and cook for another 10 minutes, until potatoes and carrots are tender. Use a colander to drain, reserving the cooking liquid. Pour the stock back into the saucepan.

In a frying pan, heat oil over medium heat, add onions and celery and sauté for 10 minutes, until tender. Transfer to a small bowl.

In the same pan, melt butter, add flour and stir for 1 minute. Carefully pour in the warm stock, stirring until smooth and thick enough to coat the back of a spoon. If it is too thick, thin with a bit more chicken stock. Stir in salt and pepper.

Add the potatoes, carrots, onions, celery and peas to the sauce. You can freeze it at this point, if you like.

CHICKEN

1 (3-lb) whole organic chicken

3 stalks celery

2 carrots

½ large onion

1 bunch Italian parsley, stems and leaves divided

6 cups water

TO FREEZE
Freeze the filled pies for up to 3 months. Bake them from frozen in a 350°F oven for 45 minutes.

PIE

3 medium-large potatoes, cut into ½-inch dice

3 large carrots, cut into ¼-inch dice

2 Tbsp vegetable oil, or as needed for sautéing

½ large onion, cut into ¼-inch dice

2 stalks celery, cut into ¼-inch dice

½ cup (1 stick) butter

¾ cup unbleached all-purpose flour

1 Tbsp sea salt

1 Tbsp ground black pepper

3 cups frozen peas

Whole-wheat flour, for dusting

4 disks chilled Pie Pastry dough (page 18), wrapped

1 egg, beaten

2 Tbsp milk or light (10%) cream

Dust the counter and the top side of a chilled pastry disk with flour and gently roll into a circle. Press together any cracks that may form at edges before and while rolling. Shift the pastry circle from time to time to prevent it from sticking to the counter. Turn pastry over, dust with more flour and roll to a ¼-inch thickness. Cut pastry circles to fit the size of the pie pans, and slightly smaller circles to be the tops. Repeat with other pastry disks as needed.

Fit pastry circles snugly into the pans. Check the gravy consistency of the filling (it should still be just thick enough to coat the back of a spoon) and add more stock if necessary. Fill each pie shell with 1 cup of filling. Place a top on each pie and press edges together with fork.

Preheat the oven to 350°F.

Beat egg and milk or cream together and lightly brush it over the pies.

Place pies on baking sheets and bake on the bottom rack for 25 minutes. Move the baking sheet to the centre rack and bake for another 15–20 minutes, until pastry is golden. Remove from the oven and serve, or set aside to cool.

Store this savoury pie in the freezer and you'll have the perfect dinner solution on hand for busy weeknights. We use the very best local beef raised ethically and organically on Salt Spring Island, and I encourage you to seek out a similar product in your own community. We also use ground beef, rather than cubed: it's got great texture and flavour, especially when mixed with all the herbs and spices. You'll need six-inch aluminum foil pie pans if you plan to freeze these.

BEEF POT PIE

MAKES 12 (6-INCH) POT PIES

In a large bowl, combine beef, onion, garlic, parsley, thyme, Worcestershire sauce, salt and pepper. Using your hands, mix ingredients together, then cover and refrigerate for 1 hour or overnight.

Pour water into medium saucepan and bring to a boil over high heat. Add carrots and cook for 10 minutes, until just tender. Drain, reserving hot liquid.

Melt butter in a large frying pan over medium-high heat, then stir in flour until the mixture sizzles, about 1 minute. Carefully pour in reserved liquid into the butter-flour mixture and whisk until smooth. Cook until it thickens. Set aside.

Heat oil in a large skillet over medium-high heat, add beef mixture and sauté for 10 minutes, until cooked through. Transfer to a large bowl, add carrots, tomatoes, peas and reserved sauce and stir until well combined. Taste and adjust seasoning if desired. Set aside to cool. (You can also freeze the filling for up to 2 months.)

3 lbs quality ground beef (not too lean)

½ onion, finely chopped

2 Tbsp crushed garlic

½ bunch Italian parsley, finely chopped

½ bunch fresh thyme, leaves only

3 Tbsp Worcestershire sauce

1 Tbsp sea salt, plus extra to taste

1 Tbsp ground black pepper, plus extra to taste

2 cups water

2 cups peeled and finely chopped carrots

½ cup (1 stick) butter

TO FREEZE

Freeze the filled pies for up to 3 months. Bake them from frozen in a 350°F oven for 45 minutes.

¾ cup unbleached
   all-purpose flour

½ cup vegetable oil

1 (796-mL) can diced
   tomatoes

2 cups frozen peas

Whole-wheat flour,
   for dusting

4 disks chilled Pie Pastry
   dough (page 18),
   wrapped

1 egg, beaten

2 Tbsp milk or light (10%)
   cream

Granna's Chili-Tomato
   Sauce (page 195),
   to serve

Dust the counter and the top side of a pastry disk with flour and gently roll into a circle. Press together any cracks that may form at edges before and while rolling. Shift the pastry circle from time to time to prevent it from sticking to the counter. Turn pastry over, dust with more flour and roll to a ¼-inch thickness. Cut the pastry circles to fit the size of the pie pans, and slightly smaller circles to be the tops. Repeat with other pastry disks as needed.

Fit pastry circles snugly into the pans and fill each shell with 1 cup of cooled filling. Place a top on each pie and press edges together with fork.

 Preheat the oven to 350°F.

Beat egg and milk (or cream) together and lightly brush it over the pies.

Place the pies on baking sheets and bake on the bottom rack for 25 minutes. Move the baking sheet to the centre rack and bake for another 15–20 minutes, until pastry is golden. Serve with Granna's Chili-Tomato Sauce.

PRESERVES AND PICKLES

M Y MOM IS the jam/chutney/sauces lady of
the Toronto Islands, and taught me
everything I know about preserving. She
gave me her best recipes, and I've included them all
here—except the one for the eggplant chutney that
Glenn Milchem, the drummer from Blue Rodeo, is
hooked on, which I promised to keep a family
secret. Preserving is a lot simpler than you might
think, so fire up your canning pot and start simmering.

THE PRESERVING PROCESS

Canning is a fun, easy way to enjoy seasonal produce year-round. But it's essential that home cooks follow certain steps to keep everything food safe.

YOU'LL NEED:

Canning pot or canner

Dishtowels

Glass jars, snap lids and screw bands

Jar lifter/tongs

Ladle

Magnetic wand (lid lifter)

Wide-mouthed funnel

THEN FOLLOW THESE THREE SIMPLE STEPS:

1 STERILIZE THE JARS

Fill a canning pot with enough water to cover the jars by at least 2 inches. Place the jars in the pot and boil for at least 10 minutes. Leave jars in the pot until you're ready to fill them and keep the water simmering. Place snap lids in a small pot of hot (not boiling) water to soften. Spread dishtowels out on the counter to set and fill jars on.

2 FILL THE JARS

Use a jar lifter to remove the jars from the canning pot. Place the funnel in each hot jar and ladle in the hot preserves, leaving ¼–½-inch headspace, then wipe the rims. Lift snap lids out of hot water using magnetic wand and towel them dry. Cover jars with the snap lids, then screw the bands on finger tight. Meanwhile, bring the water in the canning pot back up to a boil.

3 PROCESS THE JARS

Put the filled jars back into the boiling water. Keeping the water at a low boil over medium heat, process jars for 10–20 minutes, depending on the recipe. Using the lifter, remove the jars from the water and allow to cool. You'll know the lids have sealed when you hear a satisfying "pop." If you don't hear a pop and there is still a small bump on top of the snap lid, the jars have not sealed properly. Re-process those jars using new snap lids, making sure to follow all the steps. Refrigerate any jars that don't seal and consume their contents within 2 weeks.

Who doesn't love the contrast between the sweetness and vinegary tartness of bread and butter pickles? They are awesome on a cheese sandwich or a burger, or on a charcuterie plate. While any cucumbers will work in this recipe, pickling cucumbers are the best choice because they are smaller than regular cucumbers, with a softer skin, sweeter flesh and fewer seeds.

BREAD AND BUTTER PICKLES

MAKES 8–10 (500-ML) JARS

4 lbs pickling cucumbers, thinly sliced into rounds

1 large onion, thinly sliced

⅓ cup pickling salt

3 cups cider vinegar

1½ cups sugar

2 tsp mustard seeds

1 tsp turmeric powder

½ tsp celery seeds

8-10 sprigs dill (optional)

In a large bowl, combine cucumbers, onions and salt. Toss to mix, then cover and refrigerate overnight.

Drain cucumbers and onions well. In a medium stainless-steel saucepan, combine vinegar, sugar, mustard seeds, turmeric and celery seeds. Heat over medium heat until ingredients are blended.

Fill hot, sterilized jars each with a sprig a dill (if using) and the cucumber-onion mixture. Add hot pickling liquid, making sure the vegetables are covered entirely and leaving ¼–½-inch headspace. Wipe rims of jars with a clean cloth and seal. Process in canner for 10 minutes. (See page 184 for more canning info.)

Once in the jar, this marmalade has a jewel-like appearance.
I found the original recipe in a book a long time ago and since then
have restyled it a dozen times. The inclusion of carrots puzzles
people, but they just work—especially with the zing of the ginger.
It can be used just as any other jam or marmalade.

CARROT-ORANGE-GINGER MARMALADE

MAKES 8 (250-ML) JARS

Cut citrus fruit into quarters, and trim pith and remove seeds, if necessary. Put citrus quarters into a food processor and purée until smooth.

In a large stainless-steel stockpot, combine carrots, citrus purée and water. Cover and bring to a boil over medium heat. Reduce heat and simmer for 10 minutes. Stir in lemon juice, crystallized ginger, citrus zests and fresh ginger. Stir continuously at a simmer for 10 minutes.

Stir in pectin and bring to a boil. Add sugar and bring to another boil, stirring continuously until it can't be stirred down. Remove from heat, add butter and stir for 5 minutes.

Pour the mixture into hot, sterilized canning jars, leaving a ½-inch headspace. Wipe rims of jars with a clean cloth and seal. Process in canner for 15 minutes. (See page 184 for more canning info.)

3 lemons, zest coarsely grated and reserved

4 oranges, zest coarsely grated and reserved

1 lb carrots, peeled and finely grated

1 cup water

1 cup fresh lemon juice

1 cup chopped crystallized ginger

1 Tbsp freshly grated ginger

1 (170-mL) package liquid pectin (2 pouches)

5 cups sugar

1 Tbsp butter

WITH MULTISEED SPELT BREAD (PAGE 95)

This is what your Thanksgiving table has been waiting for. Mixing fresh cranberries and local apples with warming spices makes this a total fall-bounty recipe. Cran-apple sauce is perfect with turkey, either as a side for a roast or as a condiment on a sandwich.

CRAN-APPLE SAUCE

MAKES 6–8 (500-ML) JARS

Quarter orange and remove peel, pith and seeds. Purée orange slices in a food processor.

In a large stainless-steel saucepan on medium-low heat, combine orange purée with balance of ingredients. Simmer and stir frequently for 45 minutes until the mixture thickens. Remove cinnamon sticks. Taste for flavour balance and adjust if desired.

Fill hot, sterilized jars with sauce, leaving a ½-inch head-space. Wipe rims of jars with a clean cloth and seal. Process in canner for 10 minutes. (See page 184 for more canning info.)

1 orange

1½ lbs apples (about 6 large), peeled, cored and roughly chopped

2 lbs fresh or frozen cranberries (not defrosted)

2 cups sugar

2 Tbsp freshly grated ginger

Finely grated zest and juice of 1 lemon

1 tsp ground cinnamon

1 tsp ground allspice

½ tsp ground cloves

1 cup cider vinegar

1 cup chopped crystallized ginger

2 cinnamon sticks

This Caribbean-inspired chutney is super-popular and easy to make.
It's wonderfully aromatic with just a touch of heat, and perfect
with lamb patties (page 172), curries or goat cheese and crackers.

MANGO CHUTNEY

MAKES 6–8 (500-ML) JARS

5-6 fresh firm or frozen
  mangoes, coarsely
  chopped (about 6 cups)

1 cup sugar

1 cup cider vinegar

1 Tbsp freshly grated ginger

½ Tbsp ground ginger

½ Tbsp sea salt

½ Tbsp chili flakes

½ Tbsp mustard seeds

1 tsp cumin seeds

1 tsp coriander seeds

½ tsp chili powder

½ tsp turmeric powder

1 cup raisins

In a large stainless-steel stockpot on medium-low heat, combine all ingredients except the raisins. Cook, stirring often, for 30 minutes, or until thickened. Stir in raisins. Taste and adjust seasoning if desired.

Fill hot, sterilized jars with chutney, leaving a ½-inch headspace. Wipe rims of jars with a clean cloth and seal. Process in canner for 10 minutes. (See page 184 for more canning info.)

I love chutneys, and this one makes the most of local fruit in season. Chutneys originated in India, where they were traditionally simple sauces or garnishes. The tangy sweet condiment we know and love, with its combination of fresh and dried fruits with spices, was actually an Anglo-Indian invention. This version is good with pork or turkey, on sandwiches or with curry.

PEAR-APPLE CHUTNEY

MAKES 6–8 (250-ML) JARS

Combine chopped pears and apples in a large bowl and stir in lemon zest and juice.

Transfer apple-pear mixture to a large stainless-steel stockpot on medium-low heat, and add all remaining ingredients except dried cranberries. Simmer 30 minutes, stirring frequently, until the mixture has thickened. Stir in cranberries.

Pour chutney into hot, sterilized jars, leaving ½-inch headspace. Wipe rims of jars with a clean cloth and seal. Process in canner for 10 minutes. (See page 184 for more canning info.)

4 firm pears, peeled, cored and cut into ½-inch dice (about 3 cups)

4 apples, peeled, cored and cut into ½-inch dice (about 3 cups)

Finely grated zest and juice of 1 lemon

1 small onion, chopped (about ½ cup)

½ cup cider vinegar

¾ cup sugar

½ Tbsp salt

½ Tbsp ground ginger

1 tsp mustard seeds

½ tsp chili flakes

½ cup dried cranberries

Back on the Toronto Islands, after the days of the bakery cart,
my mom would make this relish for her stall at the Algonquin Island
Christmas Boutique. She's now the matriarch of the island and has
inherited the front stall at the market—she's earned it! This is one of
her most popular preserves; it's sweet and tangy, with a nice hot kick,
and excellent with chicken, pork, or cheese and crackers.

PEACH-PEPPER RELISH

MAKES 8–10 (250-ML) JARS

12 large peaches

1 Scotch bonnet pepper, chopped

12 red bell peppers, chopped

1 cup white wine vinegar

1 tsp salt

2 lemons, cut in half

4 cups sugar

Bring a saucepan of water to a boil and add peaches. Blanch for 10–30 seconds, then use a slotted spoon to transfer the peaches to a bowl of ice water. Peel, pit and chop.

In a large stainless-steel stockpot, combine chopped peaches with peppers, vinegar, salt and lemon halves and boil gently for 30 minutes.

Remove lemons and add sugar. Cook on low heat for 30 minutes, stirring, until relish has thickened.

Pour relish into hot, sterilized canning jars, leaving a ½-inch headspace. Wipe rims of jars with a clean cloth and seal. Process in canner for 10 minutes. (See page 184 for more canning info.)

Granna's spicy, tomatoey sauce is great with scrambled eggs, on a burger, with chips as a salsa, on quiche—with just about anything, really. When puréed, it makes a nice, bright, not overly spicy BBQ sauce. It simmers for an hour or more until it thickens—just be vigilant so the sugars don't burn.

GRANNA'S CHILI-TOMATO SAUCE

MAKES 6 (500-ML) JARS

SPICE BAG

½ Tbsp whole cloves

½ Tbsp whole allspice

1 cinnamon stick, broken

SAUCE

7–8 medium-large tomatoes, chopped (about 7 cups)

1 large onion, chopped (about 1 cup)

4 green bell peppers, chopped (about 2½ cups)

4 stalks celery, chopped (about 2 cups)

1 Scotch bonnet pepper, seeded and chopped

½ cup cider vinegar

½ cup packed brown sugar

2 bay leaves

½ Tbsp kosher salt

½ Tbsp ground cinnamon

½ tsp ground nutmeg

½ Tbsp mustard seeds

SPICE BAG Put all ingredients into a spice bag, or wrap in cheesecloth and tie to secure.

SAUCE Put all ingredients into a large stainless-steel stockpot on medium-low heat. Add spice bag and simmer for 1–1½ hours, stirring frequently, until the mixture has thickened.

Remove spice bag and bay leaves and pour sauce into hot, sterilized jars, leaving a ½-inch headspace. Wipe rims of jars with a clean cloth and seal. Process in canner for 10 minutes. (See page 184 for more canning info.)

METRIC CONVERSION CHART

VOLUME

IMPERIAL	METRIC
¼ tsp	1 mL
½ tsp	2.5 mL
¾ tsp	4 mL
1 tsp	5 mL
½ Tbsp	8 mL
1 Tbsp	15 mL
1½ Tbsp	23 mL
2 Tbsp	30 mL
¼ cup	60 mL
⅓ cup	80 mL
½ cup	125 mL
⅔ cup	165 mL
¾ cup	185 mL
1 cup	250 mL
1¼ cups	310 mL
1⅓ cups	330 mL
1½ cups	375 mL
1⅔ cups	415 mL
1¾ cups	435 mL
2 cups	500 mL
2¼ cups	560 mL
2⅓ cups	580 mL
2½ cups	625 mL
2¾ cups	690 mL
3 cups	750 mL
4 cups / 1 qt	1 L
5 cups	1.25 L
6 cups	1.5 L
7 cups	1.75 L
8 cups	2 L

WEIGHT

IMPERIAL	METRIC
½ oz	15 g
1 oz	30 g
2 oz	60 g
3 oz	85 g
4 oz (¼ lb)	115 g
5 oz	140 g
6 oz	170 g
7 oz	200 g
8 oz (½ lb)	225 g
9 oz	255 g
10 oz	285 g
11 oz	310 g
12 oz (¾ lb)	340 g
13 oz	370 g
14 oz	400 g
15 oz	425 g
16 oz (1 lb)	450 g
1¼ lbs	570 g
1½ lbs	670 g
2 lbs	900 g
3 lbs	1.4 kg
4 lbs	1.8 kg
5 lbs	2.3 kg
6 lbs	2.7 kg

CANS AND JARS

IMPERIAL	METRIC
14 oz	398 mL
28 oz	796 mL

LINEAR

IMPERIAL	METRIC
¼ inch	6 mm
½ inch	12 mm
¾ inch	2 cm
1 inch	2.5 cm
1¼ inches	3 cm
1½ inches	3.5 cm
1¾ inches	4.5 cm
2 inches	5 cm
2½ inches	6.5 cm
3 inches	7.5 cm
4 inches	10 cm
5 inches	12.5 cm
6 inches	15 cm
7 inches	18 cm
10 inches	25 cm
12 inches (1 foot)	30 cm
13 inches	33 cm
16 inches	41 cm
18 inches	46 cm
24 inches (2 feet)	60 cm

BAKING PANS

IMPERIAL	METRIC
9 × 13-inch cake pan	4 L cake pan
11 × 17-inch baking sheet	30 × 45-cm baking sheet

TEMPERATURE
(FOR OVEN TEMPERATURES, SEE CHART BELOW.)

IMPERIAL	METRIC
120°F	49°C
125°F	52°C
130°F	54°C
140°F	60°C
150°F	66°C
155°F	68°C
160°F	71°C
165°F	74°C
170°F	77°C
175°F	80°C
180°F	82°C
190°F	88°C
200°F	93°C
240°F	116°C
250°F	121°C
300°F	149°C
325°F	163°C
350°F	177°C
360°F	182°C
375°F	191°C

OVEN TEMPERATURE

IMPERIAL	METRIC
200°F	95°C
250°F	120°C
275°F	135°C
300°F	150°C
325°F	160°C
350°F	180°C
375°F	190°C
400°F	200°C
425°F	220°C
450°F	230°C

ACKNOWLEDGEMENTS

Baking is an act of community—you never bake for just one person, but for friends, family and neighbours. Writing a cookbook, I've discovered, is also an act of community, and that means I have many people to thank, starting with Donald Mackenzie, who motivated me to write *The Little Island Bake Shop*.

I'd also like to thank my bake shop assistants—Molly James (our most awesome student baker), Diana Cary and Alanda Nay—whose hard work allowed me to take time away from making cookies and pies to write about them instead.

Much gratitude to the hard-working farmers of Salt Spring Island, to the homeowners who so kindly bring me fruit when they have more than enough, and especially to Paul Chyz, a very gifted gardener, who has helped me to adorn many cakes with edible flowers; Susan and Dale, owners of Moby's Pub; Jeremy and Basil of the Salt Spring Inn; the wonderful staff at Salt Spring Air; and Aletha of Café Talia. Thank you. Your support means the world to me.

Working with the team at Figure 1 Publishing has been a real pleasure. Editor Michelle Meade (so patient) and copy editor Pam Robertson made the words sing and the measurements accurate. I am very grateful to Joanne Sasvari, who took me under her

wing, and for her continued guidance. I'd like to extend my gratitude to Jessica Sullivan and Naomi MacDougall as well, for their creative vision. Photographer Danielle Acken captured the sweet essence of every cake and cookie, while stylist Aurelia Louvet made each one even more beautiful than I could have imagined. Thanks, too, to Molly and Zack of Bullock Lake Farm, who loaned us their beautiful property for the shoot.

Thank you to my mom, who taught me how important it is to share good baking with the people you love. To my dad, gone so long but still always in my thoughts. To my good friends Jackie Stibbards of Merritt, with her supreme fruit-gathering skills, and Nancy Brownsell, mentor since my apprenticeship and fellow butter tart connoisseur.

Writing my story touched parts of the past, and that gave me gifts. It reconnected me with my son, Kyle, a chef who is cooking delicious things on the other side of the country. It allowed me to forgive those who needed it, and appreciate those who need it even more. And every day, it reminded me how lucky I am to have a partner like Lane, who is always there for me.

Baking is an act of community. Thank you to everyone, especially my loyal customers and fans, who are part of mine.

INDEX

ABOUT THE AUTHOR

JANA ROERICK is the owner of renowned Jana's Bake Shop, which has been serving delicious homemade desserts to the Gulf Islands for more than fifteen years. Starting with a culinary degree from George Brown College, Jana has built a successful career as a professional baker. She has also taught baking courses and workshops and is an active community supporter and fundraiser. Jana's Bake Shop has been profiled in various publications including *An Edible Journey*, *Gulf Island Driftwood* and *Aqua* magazine, and has received a Certificate of Excellence from TripAdvisor. She currently lives with her husband, Lane, and their dog, Monty, on Salt Spring Island, British Columbia.